GOD'S
STANDARD-BEARER

AN OTHER BOOK BY DR. RICK FARLEY

Attitudes of Great Leaders

AVAILABLE FROM DESTINY IMAGE PUBLISHERS

GOD'S
STANDARD-BEARER

The
TRUE MEASURE
of a
LEADER

DR. RICK FARLEY

DESTINY IMAGE® PUBLISHERS, INC.

P.O. Box 310, Shippensburg, PA 17257-0310

"Speaking to the Purposes of God for This Generation and for the Generations to Come."

This book and all other Destiny Image, Revival Press, MercyPlace, Fresh Bread, Destiny Image Fiction, and Treasure House books are available at Christian bookstores and distributors worldwide.

For a U.S. bookstore nearest you, call 1-800-722-6774.
For more information on foreign distributors, call 717-532-3040.
Reach us on the Internet: www.destinyimage.com.

ISBN 10: 0-7684-3110-7
ISBN 13: 978-0-7684-3110-0

For Worldwide Distribution, Printed in the U.S.A.
1 2 3 4 5 6 7 8 9 10 11 / 13 12 11 10 09

DEDICATION

This book is dedicated to the enduring memory of our son Jason. He was a young man whose attitude in life was an inspiration to many. Thank you God for the time that You gave him to us.

ACKNOWLEDGMENTS

I wish to express my heartfelt thanks to my wife Karren for her support and love, and to Steve Poland for all his work in proofreading the manuscript and for his many helpful suggestions.

CONTENTS

FOREWORD

If first impressions are to be trusted, the visiting evangelist had little to offer. His slight build, balding head, and scraggly beard did not present a very imposing figure. Even worse, he clearly wasn't a gifted speaker. In fact, some members of the congregation listened to his sermons with undisguised contempt.

The truth is that if the apostle Paul were to speak in the leading churches of our day, many would get up and walk out. His detractors rightly said that *"his personal presence is unimpressive and his speech contemptible"* (2 Cor. 10:10 NASB). Paul himself acknowledged that when he was in Corinth he did not preach *"with superiority of speech"* or with *"persuasive words of wisdom."* This is not a man who leaned on his own abilities. He spoke with *"weakness, in fear, and in much trembling"* (1 Cor. 2:1:4).

Immature Christians are drawn to those who are outwardly impressive. They like a leader to look the part: immaculate wardrobe, stately car, fashionable wife, and an air of self-confidence. Even more importantly, they expect ministry leaders to sound the part. People are drawn to preachers who stimulate their intellects and touch their emotions. They want to see all the trappings of visible success and be regaled by entertaining stories.

However, the Kingdom of Heaven does not operate with the same values that are so highly esteemed in our American culture. Truth be known, God does not need people with powerful personalities; He needs weak ones who know how to depend on Him. The Almighty does not need vessels full of themselves and their own talents; He needs empty vessels that can be filled with His power. The Lord does not need ministers with tremendous preaching competence; He needs people of meekness whose tongues are controlled by the Holy Spirit. A person's strengths, gifts, and capabilities are only useful to God to the degree that they have been crucified at Calvary. More often than not, a person's strength serves as God's rival, his or her ability as satan's opening.

Paul knew that the immature Christians of the Corinthian church had a very shallow perspective of God's Kingdom. To help them understand how upside down their thinking was, he shared with them a very personal struggle that he had taken to the Lord.

> *...There was given me a thorn in the flesh, a messenger of Satan to torment me—to keep me from exalting myself! Concerning this I implored the Lord three times that it might leave me. And He has said to me, "My grace is sufficient for you, for power is perfected in weakness."*
>
> *Most gladly, therefore, I will rather boast about my weaknesses, so that the power of Christ may dwell in me. Therefore I am well content with weaknesses, with insults, with distresses, with persecutions, with difficulties, for Christ's sake; for when I am weak, then I am strong* (2 Corinthians 12:7-10 NASB).

This is the key to powerful ministry that these carnal Christians did not understand. It isn't through human strength and ability that dynamic results occur. No! It is when we are weak and dependent upon the Lord that He moves most mightily. It isn't through marketing strategies that the Kingdom is built; it is through the agency of the Holy Spirit. It isn't through flattering influential people that a person is raised up for leadership; it is through quiet and humble subjection to God.

These principles are well-known to the author of this book. Richard Farley understands what it means to deal with human frailty and unspeakable loss. In fact, this very book has risen from the ash heap of tremendous personal sorrow.

God's Standard-bearer lifts up a standard for leadership that demands consideration in these last days. The unspoken message in Richard's book is this: If you are willing to pay the price to be a godly leader, then throw yourself into the great battle that is currently raging over the souls of humankind. But if you are motivated for service by some self-serving ambition, please, please choose another career. You will surely do more harm than good.

Ministry is not for those trying to make a life for themselves; it is for those who are prepared to lay down their lives for the sake of others. It is through the selfless efforts on behalf of others that God's power will be seen. Yes, it is when Christ is allowed to be all in all that victories are won and the enemy is vanquished!

Where're you ripened fields behold
Waving to God their sheaves of gold,
Be sure some corn of wheat has died,
Some saintly soul been crucified;
Someone has suffered, wept, and prayed,
And fought hell's legions undismayed.[1]

Steve Gallagher,
Pure Life Ministries

ENDNOTE

1. A.S. Booth Clibborn, quoted by Rosalind Goforth, *Jonathan Goforth* (Minneapolis: Bethany House Publishers, 1986), 121.

INTRODUCTION

A young man, Mr. Sights, is seated in a still, quiet foyer of an office building, anxiety fluttering through him as he repeatedly takes anxious glances toward a door across from him. His beautiful young wife slips her hand between his tapping fingers, touches his knee, and smiles at him. They interlock fingers in a gentle loving squeeze while he continues to tap his foot. He returns a fleeting smile and then looks back to the door.

After what feels like an eternity the door swings open and another man dressed in a suit waves them into the intimidating room. Seven men, also all in suits, are seated around a long, glossy conference table. Their smiles do little to calm the young man as he and his wife are directed to take the two empty chairs at the table.

Seated at the head of the table, a distinguished looking man in his late fifties pensively flips through several pages of a stack of papers in front of him. The distinguished man, Bishop Decision, chairman of the District Credentialing Committee, looks up from his perusal and smiles as he slides the stack of papers across the glossy table to the gentleman next to him. Mr. Sights recognizes the cover page of the pack of papers as his application and recommendations to this esteemed committee board.

Mr. and Mrs. Sights settle into their seats and the Bishop warmly greets them as he lays his glasses on the glossy table. To Mr. Sights it sounds like a rock landing on the table.

"I've looked over your application, Mr. Sights, and I am a little concerned about how you answered question four," Bishop Decision begins. "Could you explain your reasoning to us?"

The Bishop's voice soundes muffled and miles away through Sights's clamoring anxiety. The other gentleman slides the application across the table. Sights hopes his hand does not tremble as he reaches out to receive the sliding papers.

His hand does tremble ever so slightly as he looks up at the array of suits and tries to smile. Everyone is locked onto his face with an expectant gaze. One of them lowers his head to write something down. Mr. Sights gathers his thoughts, takes a deep breath, steels himself with the poise he knows he has, and answers the question with confidence.

Relieved that they are apparently satisfied with his answer, he is further relieved when one of the other board members looks at his wife and asks, "How do you feel, Mrs. Sights, about your husband's call to ministry?"

She starts to respond when the board member continues, "Do you understand the trials a pastor's wife will need to endure?"

"Yes, sir, I do. I truly believe in my husband's call."

Resuming his role in the interview process, the Bishop looks back at Mr. Sights. "In your own words, Mr. Sights," the Bishop requests, "tell us why you believe you are called by God."

The process continues for 15 or 20 minutes. The committee then asks the young minister and his wife to leave the room while the board discusses their answers and considers their request for credentials.

This process is repeated many times throughout the year across the nation by many different church organizations. The reason is to safeguard the believers who will be following the ministry of men and women who feel called by God. Unfortunately this safeguard is not a guarantee in our day.

Today a man or woman can go on the Internet and receive an ordination in the time it takes to type in an address. Then there are those that will ordain you by mail sight unseen and doctrine unknown.

I recall a visit by a man who asked if our church would ordain him. When I explained to him that it would take three years to complete the process of ordination, he answered, "No thanks. I'll go search for someone else who will ordain me now."

My wife, Karren, asked if I had seen a news broadcast concerning a minister being arrested for solicitation. She continued by stating that he had been arrested for soliciting a male undercover police officer for prostitution. It seems that he preached adamantly against homosexuality while secretly indulging in the homosexual lifestyle himself.

These improprieties cause little surprise in today's church world, where sexual sins are more and more frequent. Whether it is a priest molesting a young child, or a television minister involved in adultery or pornography, it seems that the church world is guilty of the same indulgences as everyone else.

Sexual sins are only the tip of the iceberg. Fleecing the flock, deceiving the innocent, and many other sins abound. Many design their own concepts of God and Christ. However, when we design a god or set our own standards for God outside of the Word of God, then He ceases to be God and we take God's place. When man designs God, man does exactly what lucifer did to cause his fall from grace.

The real question is not, Are these truly men and women of God, or are they wolves in sheeps' clothing? Rather, it should be, *Does God have His own standard for those who lead?* Does God have a standard that would disqualify someone from leading His church body?

How can you tell what is real and what is false? Are you sitting in a church that is full, yet being led astray by a disqualified leader? Does God really disqualify? Is the church existing to entertain you or to train you in the ways of God and the Christian life? Should the preacher be a parapsychologist, or should he or she preach the cross? Is church leadership measured in congregational numbers? Can we disqualify ourselves?

In this day and age of megachurches and international TV ministries, what measure does God use? Does He still use the plumbline spoken about in the Old Testament to test our lives? If God allows us to devise our own standards for ministry, what about Revelation chapters 1-3 where He judges each church by His standards of ministry?

In the following pages I will answer these and many other questions concerning what God says about leadership. In our age of permissiveness and political correctness, the only way to know what God says about leadership is by God's own standards, not a denomination's standard or the media or what the church across the street has to say on the issue.

The Dream

Recently I had a dream concerning the church. In this dream I was standing outside a church building at the entrance. However, the entrance was blocked by a large bomb. There were wires running from the bomb around the church in both directions. These wires were attached to more bombs placed at each entrance to the church building.

The bomb in front of me had a timer attached to it and it was counting down quickly. Then the voice of the Lord spoke to me in the dream and said, "The combination is 721." I bent down and punched in the numbers 721 on the keypad. When I did this the timer stopped and the wires fell loose from all the bombs. The church was saved from the destruction that the enemy had intended.

I got up out of bed and went to another room and wrote down the numbers 721 so I would remember them in the morning.

When morning came I got up and went on the Internet to try and find out if there was anything special about the numbers 721. This effort failed to give me any insight into what God was saying to me in the dream. However, I had recently bought a book entitled *Understanding the Dreams You Dream* by Ira Milligan, and the author included a section on numbers.[1] It defined 7 but there was no definition of the number 21. Fortunately he had listed his phone number in the front of the book. I dialed it and was surprised when he answered the phone immediately.

Reverend Milligan was very helpful and explained how the numbers and multiplication of numbers work. The number *7* is God's number of completion, *20* represents holy or holiness, and the number *1* represents a new beginning.

So 721 in my dream means *a complete holy beginning for the church*. Rev. Milligan stated that since God had revealed that the combination was 721, He is saying to attain this new beginning, we need to preach more holiness.[2]

A return to holiness is a necessity today. Hebrews 12:14 says, *"Follow peace with all men, and holiness, without which no man shall see the Lord"* (KJV). The first priority for ministry is not education or denominational affiliation. The first mandate for serving God and leading others is a holy life and walking with the God you serve.

I trust you will see in the following pages what God expects of us as leaders. We will look at those who were called by God and the principles and standards set by Him for ministry in the Word of God.

Endnotes

1. Ira Milligan, *Understanding the Dreams You Dream* (Shippensburg, PA: Treasure House, 1997).

2. Phone conversation between the author and Reverend Ira Milligan, January 2008.

CHAPTER 1

THE BEGINNING

An old man with long white hair and a long flowing beard laboriously made his way down a rocky, precipitous mountain. Further hindering his tenuous descent over jagged outcroppings of rock were two large stone slabs he lugged with him. The baking sun shone against the dark rock background and pressed Moses with heat as the wind whipped his long hair and beard.

His face bore the deep thought and wisdom one would no doubt have, had he or she just spent the last 40 days and 40 nights on top of a mountain face to face with God. *On these stone slabs is the law of God,* he thought with incredulous awe. The reality of the thought caused Moses's arms to tighten around the precious slabs, now clutched even tighter to his torso.

Moses has had the rarest experience of any man living on the earth. He has spent 40 days in a one-on-one encounter with the God of the Universe. God has shared His will with him. God has given him the specific designs of a tabernacle of worship: every detail of the furniture, the worship, and the laws of government.

Moses was God's messenger, carrying with him the handiwork of God's own hand, the ten laws written by God to govern His covenant people Israel. Even though he hadn't eaten for 40 days and was weak, he hurried rather recklessly. God had said, in essence, "Hurry and get down because the people are sinning" (see Exod. 32:7). Moses had stood in the gap for Israel and pleaded with God not to destroy them. God had relented in his wrath as Moses had interceded. Now Moses had to get down as fast as possible and put an end to the sin.

Stepping around the steep slope to the face of the mountain, still weighed down by the Ten Commandments written on stone slabs, Moses saw Israel in the distance below, and vaguely heard shouting from the people there. Joshua, who had been left on the mountainside, came running to Moses.

"That's the noise of war in the camp!" Joshua cried.

"It's not the noise of victory," said Moses. "Nor is it the noise of the cry of defeat. It's the sound of singing I hear," he said dubiously (see Exod. 32:18).

With the cloud of God still hovering overhead as it had since they crossed the Red Sea, Moses stood on a ledge and peered over at the camp below. Thousands of tents stretched out before him for what seemed like a mile.

A large crowd had gathered over to the north of the camp. They were dancing and shouting with glee, engaged in a swilling drunken party around the statue of a golden calf. Enraged over what he was seeing, Moses lifted the stone tablets of God over his head and dashed them against the rocks breaking them in pieces. No longer encumbered by the inscribed laws of God on the stone, his approach to the camp was swift in anger.

He took the golden calf the people had made and melted it down, grinding it to powder, scattered it upon the water, and made the people drink the water. Moses then called out to Israel and said, *"Whoever is on the Lord's side—come to me!"* (Exod. 32:26). And all the sons of Levi gathered themselves together to him. He then sent the Levites into the camp to execute those who engaged in this sin.

According to the book of Exodus, God began to dictate to Aaron and his family what they were to do to answer the call of the High Priest for Israel. God chose the Levites as His own because they were willing to separate and stand with Moses against sinful Israel. They were chosen as the ministers of the tabernacle and keepers of its articles of worship. They were to serve in different capacities: singing, playing music, taking down the Tabernacle, carrying it and its furnishings, and helping the priest to fulfill his capacities.

However, God did not leave them without regulations concerning priests and their office. As we proceed to God's regulations for the descendents of Aaron and their ministries, it is important to understand that everything God told Moses was meant to be followed to the letter.

Now some are thinking, *That's all Old Testament. Jesus came to fulfill the law! Let's stick to the New Testament.* In answer to that, we need to look at the words of Jesus Himself in Matthew 5:17: *"Do not think that I came to destroy the Law or the Prophets. I did not come to destroy but to fulfill."*

Jesus says He didn't come to destroy the law. He just came to take off the covering of corruption that the religious leaders had placed over it: to remove the traditions, rules, creeds, and regulations that the religious had placed on it. Jesus fulfilled the ceremonial aspects of the law, but the moral and life-giving precepts of it are alive today. Jesus was the sacrifice needed by the ceremonial law. Jesus knew that the only thing that could break through the traditions of religion was the truth!

He did not come to deny its validity, to abolish the truths, to deny its inspiration or authority. This is what religion has done today. It has taken parts of the Bible and annulled its authority and power in people's lives.

To fulfill means that He came to substantiate, to make good what was announced. He verified the substance of the shadow. Substance is needed to fulfill the shadow, not destroy it—just as summer does not destroy spring, it just fulfills it. The New Testament doesn't dissolve the Old; it just takes you from doing it yourself to doing it with Jesus.

Jesus revealed that the Old Testament was still relevant in the wilderness by gaining victory over satan through His words. He said, "It is written." Where was it written? It was written in the Old Testament. He proved the authority of the Old by using it to defeat satan. His teachings recorded in the New Testament quote out of 24 Old Testament books. He quoted passages from Genesis to Deuteronomy 66 times, from Isaiah alone 40 times, plus many times from the Psalms. If He came to destroy the Old Testament, would He have been quoting it that much? He did not come to destroy, to annul, or to take away its inspiration.

This is what religion has done today. The religious have taken parts of the Bible and annulled its authority and power over our lives. The Bible is the Book of the Church, not a creed, not a book of bylaws, but the Word of God!

Jesus came to fulfill the law! He is saying, "I have come to substantiate, to make good what was announced. I came to say it's good, it's real, it's inspired. I came to rescue it from the false covering given by the religious leaders, to rescue it from the false interpretations and explain its higher meaning. I came to rescue it from the corruption of human traditions."

The New Testament doesn't dissolve the Old; it just negates the need for you to do it yourself and allows you to doing it with Jesus.

While these Scriptures were literal for Aaron and his descendents, they supply us with types or allegories for the New Testament Church today. God does have a standard and He wants us to know what He expects from those called to ministry. The Old Testament standard was meant to represent Christ—to be a type of His perfection. In the New Testament we realize that God's *spiritual* standard has not changed, even if the *physical* has changed.

For example, God no longer says that handicapped people cannot serve in ministerial capacities. It is important to understand in this first chapter that God no longer holds to the physical standard—this was a type illustrating God's spiritual standard today. I have had the privilege of sitting under some truly great ministers of the Gospel including ministers who were blind and preached from a Braille Bible, who had been handicapped by polio, who were battling MS, who stuttered, and who had been born small in stature. None of these handicaps hindered the anointing upon their lives as they ministered for God.

So realize that this book is not a statement that any of the physical attributes listed by God as disqualifying Levites from the priesthood apply physically in this dispensation of grace.

REVIEW QUESTIONS

1. What was the rare experience that Moses had with God that no one else has ever had?

2. What event caused God to choose Levi and his descendants as His people?

3. What parts of the law are relevant today?

4. Jesus came to fulfill the law. What does that mean?

CHAPTER 2

GOD PLACES RULES ON THE LEVITES

The author of the Book of Hebrews made several statements about our lives in Christ—statements like, "*...that we may be partakers of His holiness*" and "*...holiness, without which no one will see the Lord*" (Heb. 12:10,14). The apostle Peter stated, "Because it is written, 'Be holy, for I am holy'" (1 Pet. 1:16).

This and many other statements in the Word of God lead us to believe that holiness is the one of the highest attributes that God manifests. In the Old Testament anyone who had not been cleansed (sanctified) and made holy could not approach the presence of God.

We read of Aaron's two sons who crossed that line of holiness. They saw the fire come out from the tabernacle of God and burn up the offering (see Lev. 10:1-3). It seems evident that they had been drinking because of the law that was enacted immediately following their actions. But in their drunken state they took it upon themselves to intrude into the priest's office uninvited by God, using strange fire to burn incense before God.

This presumption, whether by pride or drunkenness, led to their deaths. Fire came out of the tabernacle and devoured them. One thing that is certain from this incident is that there is a right way and a wrong way to enter God's presence. It is not something given to us to decide but to be done under God's directions.

The ministry of the tabernacle had been set up by God. Moses and Aaron had come from the Levite family known as the Kohath family. God assigned this family the duties of taking care of the most holy things designed for the tabernacle. The other two families of Levites were given other duties for the care of the tabernacle and the worship of God.

All the Levites were now ministers of God chosen by Him as His people, separated from the rest of the body of Israel. The high priest could come into the presence of God in His holiness only once a year, and that was not because he chose to, but because God chose him and cleansed him for that purpose.

When it comes to ministry, it is not our choosing; it is His calling that makes it possible. We do not need self-called men and women trying to serve God. We need called people, anointed by God for the work of the ministry, not professionals who chose the ministry as an occupation. Mother and dad can't call you, the church can't call you; it must be God who calls you to the life of holiness.

> *Just as He chose us in Him before the foundation of the world, that we should be **holy** and **without blame** before Him in love"* (Ephesians 1:4, emphasis added).

You will notice that God never calls us to be like Him in His omnipotence, omniscience, or omnipresence. But He does call us to His holiness in order to approach Him. We would have to be a god to be omnipotent, omniscient, and omnipresent, but He evidently created us to be able to be like God in holiness!

I know that God never asks of us anything that is impossible for us to do. I can be holy because He is holy. His holiness comes to me and pours into me through His Son and His work. I believe God requires holiness because He desires to live within us. He has chosen His people to be a holy habitation for Him. The Holy Spirit dwells within us, and according to the Word, He is an agent of sanctification helping to produce holiness. His presence in us helps to make us holy. Just think, we are the only creatures on this earth that God has chosen to carry His Holy Spirit within!

Over the years I have been asked, "What is holiness?"

My answer to this question is: Holiness is not whether you are manifesting all the gifts of the Spirit. If you see a man on the street raising the dead or healing the sick, this does not mean he is holy. Exercising the gifts of the Spirit is the right of even the youngest believer. The signs of a holy life to me are found in Galatians 5:22-23. A person is holy who is manifesting the character or fruit of the Holy Spirit in his or her everyday life. It is determined by how we work and how we treat our brethren in our everyday life.

I have seen people who were disqualified from ministry by the words of their own mouths and yet who preach with what seems to be a great anointing. Souls come to the altar and people get healed in the prayer line. One time when I knew a person was swindling God's people, I told God I couldn't understand how this could be happening. The Spirit spoke to me in that still small voice and said, "My Word will not return void, no matter who declares it."

Watch and you will see His personal fruit manifest. Never judge a ministry or person by who comes to the altar when he preaches or by the bodies that are healed when he prays because it is God's Spirit who draws people unto Him. And it is God's

Word and people's faith that obtain healing. God saves, heals, and delivers, not people.

Matthew 7:21-23 says:

> *Not everyone who says to Me, "Lord, Lord," shall enter the kingdom of heaven, but he who does the will of My Father in heaven. Many will say to Me in that day, "Lord, Lord, have we not prophesied in Your name, cast out demons in Your name, and done many wonders in Your name?" And then I will declare to them, "I never knew you; depart from Me, you who practice lawlessness!"*

Prophesying in His name, casting out demons in His name, and doing wonders are not a sign of holiness. Yet today's church society may idolize ministers because of these signs, while not knowing anything about their lives.

Ephesians 4:17-32 speaks of holiness in its simplest form: putting off the old nature and putting on the new nature created in God. Holiness is telling the truth instead of lying. Holiness is ceasing to steal, getting a job, and helping others. It's changing the way you talk to others and the language you use. It is treating people with genuine respect.

God's command in Isaiah 52:11 to the priesthood is, "...*Be ye clean, that bear the vessels of the Lord*" (KJV). Holiness in life and character was important in the priesthood. In the book of Leviticus God set down many standards for the work and lives of the priesthood. But in Leviticus 21:17-21 God gave a list of those who were not qualified to serve as priests, even if they were a part of the proper Levitical family lineage.

> *Speak unto Aaron, saying: "No man of your descendants in succeeding generations, who has any defect* [blemish], *may approach to offer the bread of his God. For any man who has a defect* [blemish] *shall not approach: a man blind or lame, who has a marred face or any limb too long, a man who has a broken foot or broken hand, or is a hunchback or a dwarf, or a man who has a defect in his eye, or eczema or scab, or is a eunuch. No man of the descendants of Aaron the priest, who has a defect, shall come near to offer the bread of his God."*

The priest took great care in the sacrifices to make sure that they were without blemish. The reason was because they had to represent the perfection of Christ. Even the inside of the skins had to be checked to make sure it was without blemish. Because Christ was the perfect sacrifice for our sins, He Himself knew no sin—or had no spiritual blemish. This mandated that the one making the sacrifice, the priest, had to be without physical blemish as well.

In the next chapters we will discuss the blemishes that God said disqualifies a person from serving as a priest or minister in His service. These blemishes removed men from leadership and service in all capacities to God.

Avon Mentality

Today we have an "Avon mentality" in the church world. In the last chapter of Job we find that Job listed his three daughters by name and yet did not list his seven sons. This is unusual, as often in the Bible the sons are listed and the daughters are not. Job 42:13-14 says, *"He also had seven sons and three daughters. And he called the name of the first Jemimah, the name of the second Keziah, and the name of the third Keren-Happuch."*

This intrigued me, so I looked to see why this unusual situation happened. I found that the secret is in the names of the daughters. *Jemimah* means "the dove," *Keziah* means "the stripping off of the bark," and *Keren-Happuch* means "the horn of cosmetics" or "eye shadow."

What was Job trying to convey to us? He was telling his story in the names of his daughters. First, Job was recognizing that the Spirit of God had allowed all that had befallen Job for the purpose of destroying or killing his outer man of pride and self-righteousness. When you strip the bark off a tree, you are killing it; it will not survive without its bark. So Job is saying, in essence, "The Holy Spirit came to strip off my bark, so I would die." Just as Paul tells us to crucify the old man in Romans and to put off the old man in Ephesians, Job tells us that his old man was dead, crucified with Jesus (see Rom. 6:6; Eph. 4:22).

THE COSMETIC

Then Job tells us the reasons for this action of the Holy Spirit. God had to remove the cosmetics out of Job's life!

Cosmetics are those things that we use to cover our blemishes so that others cannot see them. Just as people stand in front of the mirror every morning applying cosmetics to make themselves look better to others, the church endeavors to cover its blemishes by outward cosmetics. God doesn't accept those with blemishes in His leadership. What God asks for is that we repent of our sins rather than hide them.

Another example is found in First Kings 14:25-28 where we read that Shishak, the king of Egypt (a type of satan), came up against Jerusalem and took away the treasure of the house of the Lord and all the shields of gold that Solomon had made. (These shields hung on the walls of the temple and would shine in the sunlight.) Rehoboam, the king of Judah, replaced them with brass shields that he had made. They still appeared to shine as gold from a distance, but beneath the surface was blemished, inferior metal. Gold speaks of the divine while brass symbolizes judgment.

It may have looked the same from the distance, but nonetheless, there was quite a difference. It was cosmetic. The real gold was gone from the house of God. The divine was missing! The people were living with the cosmetic, perhaps saying, "Look, it still looks as good!" But phony is phony. God wants the cosmetic faith removed from our lives and His Church. God's standard is gold (holiness unto the Lord).

Jesus's cry in Revelation 3:18 is, "I counsel you to buy from Me gold refined in the fire…." The church in these last days is still substituting programs and entertainment to replace true anointing. ***God's standards do not change with time!***

In Second Samuel 6 we read the story of King David's desire to bring the Ark of the Covenant to Jerusalem. The Ark was placed upon a brand new cart and oxen. The Israelites started out with a great celebration. Music was played upon all manner of instruments. Then the oxen stumbled and the cart shook. The Ark began to tilt, so a Levite named Uzzah reached up to steady it. When he touched the Ark, he fell over dead—evidently struck down by God himself.

Why? Because they were violating God's standards. Standards that He had set over 400 years before in the law given to Moses. God had instructed that the only way the Ark was to be moved was on the shoulders of Levites. They were to cover it and place wooden staves through rings on the Ark and place it upon their shoulders.

Why would God strike down Uzzah 400 years after a law was given? Because when God sets a standard He expects it to be obeyed—regardless of how much time has passed. You may say, "We are in the 21st century and that was written thousands of years ago." God does not change His standard because culture or civilizations change. His call for holiness in ministry has never changed!

REVIEW QUESTIONS

1. What is the one of the highest attributes of God mentioned in this chapter?

2. What did you learn about holiness in ministry in this chapter?

3. What concept of holiness did you draw from the chapter?

4. How do you define your concept of holiness?

5. What is an "Avon mentality"?

Chapter 3

FIRST STANDARD FOR SERVICE

"For any man who has a defect shall not approach: a man blind…."—Leviticus 21:18

I remember so well my years as a teenager working for my church. Our church was in a massive building program. We had outgrown our building and we were building a new extension with a wraparound balcony. I was 15 and working after school at the church to earn some spending money.

Pastor Miles, a man in his early 40s, was a man of vision who had come to the Cumberland Valley to start a church years earlier. My father, who was an evangelist, had come home one day and said, "I have found the church I want the kids to grow up in while I travel." Within weeks we had moved from southern West Virginia to Maryland. That was the kind of effect this pastor could have on a man. By my teenage years the church overflowed with people, due largely to the love this man showed to everyone around him.

The amazing thing about Pastor Miles was that he was legally blind. During the building program he came walking into the building one day to check on the progress. I remember speaking to him and walking to within one foot of him before he could recognize who I was. The church hired drivers to take him wherever he needed to go because he couldn't see to drive. But he could preach the Word! His ministry produced ten other pastors that I know of, plus missionaries to the Philippines, South America, India, Africa, and elsewhere. I remember crowds of over 1,000 people and revivals that lasted six and seven weeks. Pastor Miles changed my life and helped mold me for the ministry. His handicap didn't matter or affect any of us in a negative way. We had no doubt he was an anointed man of God.

So why would God tell Aaron that the first blemish to disqualify a man from leadership was blindness?

In his book *Holiness,* Dr. Alex Ness states:

> A blind person needs someone else to lead them. God's priests must not be led about by every wind of doctrine; they are to lead the blind. A blind person walking alone must depend upon other keen senses. He learns to go

> by touch, by feeling. The priest to properly officiate, must examine the sacrifice to see if it is without blemish. He must see the one who offered the sacrifice and see if he is sincerely repentant. A blind man walks in uncertainty. He cannot see the sun, "SON" in all the glory and beauty and walk in the light thereof.[1]

When Jesus spoke of the blind leading the blind He was speaking of the spiritually blind Pharisees who were leading other spiritually blind people.

Blindness speaks of those whose judgment has been corrupted. The term *blind* is used of those who are blind to the truth of salvation, those who are conceited and puffed up by success, and ministers who are ignorant. I am particularly drawn to the books written by the apostle John because he makes his statements so plain and understandable that it is really hard to misinterpret them. In First John 2:11 he says, *"But he who hates his brother is in darkness and walks in darkness, and does not know where he is going, because the darkness has blinded his eyes."*

Walking in jealousy and unforgiveness means that we are blinded by our emotions. Because hating your brother means you are spiritually blind. Your excuses are just your way of trying to use your other senses because you cannot see in the darkness of your heart.

A blind leader was disqualified because he could not discern what was sin and what was not. Who sets the standard? Is it the world? Is it other successful ministries, or is it God? The standard is set by the Word of God, not by what the crowd wants, or what the church down the street does, or how good it feels.

He who is blind cannot see his own condition, any imminent danger, or his need of a savior! Glasses won't help. Correcting his vision with education and culture won't help. None of these can reach the root problem—the natural person is born blind spiritually.

King Saul is an excellent example of this point. He was called and anointed to be king by God. His leadership was accepted by the people and he was called to serve Israel as their king.

Then he came to a place of decision: Should he do what God instructed him to do or what the people wished? (See 1 Samuel 15:14-24.) Saul's choice was to obey the voice of the people. In leadership we need to keep our focus on "the needs of the people and not the need to please the people." In this case Saul listened to the people and kept the best animals alive, after God had told him to destroy everything. Therefore, by God's standards, he disqualified himself from his leadership position. Pleasing God requires obedience and submission to God. Pleasing people displays weak leadership.

What did God do? He disqualified Saul and went to find a new leader for Israel. To Israel nothing changed and Saul continued to lead them. But God had removed his anointing and calling. This leaves us with another question. Are there men and women in leadership today who have been disqualified by God, without the people's knowledge, who have become blind to the sins of the world and the sins that are allowed into the church? "...*Having their understanding darkened, being alienated from the life of God, because of the ignorance that is in them, because of the blindness of their heart*" (Eph. 4:18).

We need God to open our eyes to see beyond the world, beyond the media, beyond all those things that have blinded us to the truth of serving God and His demand for holiness!

We can become so consumed with life, circumstances, leadership, and problems, that we are blinded to what is around us and blinded to the truth of what God sees. In Second Kings 6:8-23, Elisha was surrounded by the Syrian army at the town of Dothan. His servant rose early and saw the enemy army surrounding them and was frightened.

The servant ran in the house and woke Elisha and brought him out to see the army that had come after him. Just think, an army of thousands to catch one man of God! Well, Elisha wasn't shaken at all. He saw with eyes that his servant didn't possess. The servant was blind to the spiritual truth, "...those who are with us are more than those who are with them." The circumstances of the situation had consumed the servant's vision. Then Elisha prayed, "Lord, I pray, open his eyes that he may see." Only then did this young servant see God's solution to the situation.

In the Gospel of Luke, following the crucifixion of Christ, two disciples were walking on the road to Emmaus. They were so consumed with grief and disappointment that they did not recognize Jesus as He walked with them. It was only after He broke bread with them that the Bible says, *"Then their eyes were opened and they knew Him..."* (Luke 24:31).

One other incident is the story of Hagar, the mother of Ishmael, in Genesis 21. She and her son Ishmael were cast out of Abraham's home at the insistence of Sarah. Abraham gave them water and bread and sent them on their way. After a while their supplies were depleted and they became dehydrated in the desert heat. Hagar laid her son down under a bush and went a distance away so she would not see him die. There she cried out in anguish. Suddenly an angel spoke to her and asked her, *"What ails you, Hagar? Fear not..."* the angel instructed. Then ***God opened her eyes,*** and she saw a well of water.

The well of water was there all the time. But Hagar was so consumed with grief and fear, she could not see the answer was right before her eyes. Leaders can allow spiritual blindness to creep into their lives in many different ways. Perhaps attacks by other believers, disappointments, circumstances they could not control, anger with God, or just plain lack of true faith can creep in.

We lose our vision and our God-given perspectives. The only answer is the prayer, "Lord, open my eyes, cure my blindness, let me see things with a God-given perspective. Help me see sin for what it is! Don't let me be blinded by the world or by my desires!"

One of the prerequisites given by Elijah for Elisha to move into his prophetic ministry was *"if you see me when I am taken from you"* (see 2 Kings 2:10). Elijah tried three times to convince Elisha to stay behind while he went to meet God. Each time he failed, because Elisha knew that God was going to take Elijah to Heaven that day and he wanted something before Elijah left.

After they had crossed the Jordan River, Elijah asked Elisha what he wanted. Elisha replied, "I want double what you have!" Elijah didn't say no. His reply was, "If you are able to see me when I go, then you can have what you ask." The rest of the sons of the prophets, who stood over on the hillside, saw Elijah taken up by a tornado and thought he was thrown somewhere in the mountains

But Elisha saw the truth; his eyes were open. He saw the fiery chariot of the Lord coming down the road and separating him from Elijah. Because he was able to see and was not blind to the spiritual, he received double the power. Some leaders are so consumed with the past and their failures that they can't see the future, creating a form of blindness.

I was working as a manager in retail security, my first job after the Army, when I saw a man putting unpaid merchandise in his shirt. He proceeded to leave the department and headed for the exit. I followed him, planning to arrest him after he left the store. But he stopped short of the doors and looked around to see if anyone was following him. I walked on past and headed out the doors as if I was just another customer. I kept glancing back to see if he was following. He proceeded toward the doors and I kept on walking. I walked outside and glanced back to see if he was following. When I looked back I ran straight into a metal post smacking my head hard—it nearly knocked me out. His arrest was without incident, because he was laughing so hard I doubt he could have run if he wanted to!

The object of this story is to illustrate the fact that when you are consumed with what is behind, you are blind to what is before you. You cannot follow your vision if you are constantly looking back.

Realize the author of blindness is satan. Second Corinthians 4:4 states, "...*whose minds the god of this age has blinded, who do not believe....*"

God disqualifies the spiritually blind but empowers those who will open their eyes to His ways. Spiritual blindness seems to be an obvious reason for God to disqualify a leader.

However many of the other reasons are not as obvious, as will be seen in the following chapters.

ENDNOTE

1. Dr. Alex W. Ness, *Holiness* (Canada: Moriah Publications Inc., Formerly Agapre Publications, 2006), 128. Used by permission. www.MoriahPublications .com.

REVIEW QUESTIONS

1. Why would God tell Moses that a blind man could not serve?

2. Can life's circumstances cause you to become spiritually blind?

3. Why do you think Elijah made the condition of anointing "if you see me when I go"?

Chapter 4

THOSE WHO ARE LAME

"For any man who has a defect shall not approach: a man...lame...."—Leviticus 21:18

A priest enters the courtyard and walks towards the brazen alter. He is walking with a cane because he is lame in one foot. He balances himself on his cane while he tries to sacrifice an ox. He has to have help as he is cutting the animal into portions for the ritual.

Later that day he has to handle the heave offering for the first fruits offering, but he is unable to wave the heave offering before the Lord and hold onto his cane. He soon falls with the bundle of wheat falling on top of him. We can see why it would be difficult for a lame man to perform the functions of the priesthood.

A man had to be without handicap in the Old Testament rituals in order to perform the duties of a priest. Being lame was one of the disqualifying handicaps that removed him from being able to serve God in this way.

I remember 45 years ago, while attending high school, I developed a problem with my foot. It became very sore and difficult to walk on. When taking gym class I would fall behind because my lame foot would cause me to limp. Running was a real problem because I would always fall behind and come in last. Each step would send pain up the nerves of my leg. A trip to the doctor's office soon corrected the problem. I had evidently stepped on something very small that had worked its way under the skin on the bottom of my foot.

Thinking back I can see how lameness in my foot caused me to step unevenly, changed my gait as I walked, and caused me to fall behind those I tried to walk beside. If they wanted to stay with me they had to slow down and remain behind the others. Therefore my lameness not only affected me but also affected my friends.

In the Old Testament those who were lame could not serve in the house of God. It was impossible to carry the heave offerings, hold and slay the sacrifices, carry oil for the lamp, or swing the censer with incense before the altar while encumbered with a cane or crutches.

In today's society we have a number of uses for the term *lame*. You can be called lamebrained, or what you have to say is called "lame." You can be a lame individual or a lame-duck president! All of these statements imply that you are coming up short or that you are going to be non productive.

Dr. Ness in his book *Holiness* states:

> A lame priest would not symbolize Him whose *legs are as pillars of marble* (Song of Solomon 5:15), and saints who are to stand firm as pillars in the house of God. A lame man cannot walk straight. Saints are to *walk worthy* of the Lord (Col. 1:10) and are to walk even as Jesus walked.
>
> *"He that saith he abideth in Him ought himself also so to walk, even as He walked"* (1 John 2:6 KJV).[1]

The lame man's walk is uneven. It is up and down. The believer is to be consistent in his or her walk, not up today and down tomorrow. His step is uncertain and he falls easily in inclement weather. Why are there so many spiritually lame Christians? They are up and down, and most are down more often than up. They are so uncertain of their footing. They are not sure of their standing in Christ.

Feet that are *"shod...with the preparation of the gospel of peace"* (Eph. 6:15) are able to stand in the greatest battles. The feet that are lighted by the Word are beautiful as they carry those who preach the Gospel (see Rom. 10:15). *"Your word is a lamp to my feet and a light to my path"* (Ps. 119:105).

In my book *Attitudes of Great Leaders* I discussed the fact that feet represent our authority in the Gospel. One reason you can come up lame is due to having the wrong shoes or an object in your shoes that doesn't belong there, such as a stone or sand.

If your shoes are the wrong size then you will rub a blister on your foot and become lame. Your spiritual feet are supposed to be shod with the Gospel of Peace so that you can walk an even path for God and practice the Word. The Bible calls it walking circumspectly.

There are those who are coming up lame today, because they have added to the Gospel or they have put the wrong gospel shoes on their feet. Some are wearing a gospel of New Age origins. Perhaps even older than that: a gospel from the plains of Babylon, getting its origins from Nimrod the hunter of souls before the lord (see Gen. 10:8-9).

Is a faith that welcomes all religions, teaching that all paths lead to God, a gospel fit for the feet of the Church? No! When we teach that all paths or religions lead to God, we are advocating polytheism or pantheism (that God is in everything, or that all gods are the same).

Most religions have something in common in the area of ethics. They all agree that we should live circumspectly, that we should refrain from stealing, cheating, lying, lust, greed, murder, adultery, etc. Most also teach that we should live at peace with one another and treat others as we ourselves would like to be treated. Beyond this point there is little in common! Two main beliefs make different religions poles apart: how to obtain salvation and what kind of existence we can expect after death.

Christianity teaches that the only way salvation can be obtained is by the grace or unmerited favor of God. Christianity is not man reaching up to God. It's God reaching down to man with His gift.

It was God who gave His only begotten Son, that the world might believe on Him and be saved. It was Jesus who said, *"I am the way, the truth, and the life. No one comes to the Father except through Me"* (John 14:6).

There is only one name to which every knee shall bow down! That's the name of God's only begotten son, Jesus Christ. *"Nor is there salvation in any other, for there is no other name under heaven given among men by which we must be saved"* (Acts 4:12).

I was talking to a young man one day about his pastor and asked if the church sold tapes of his sermons. I told him I would like to hear him preach. He hesitated for about one minute and said, "I just can't describe his kind of preaching to you." He continued saying that the pastor would cause believers who have been saved for any period of time to drop their mouths in surprise because of his unique speaking style. "He doesn't speak like you're used to hearing. There are a lot of frightened people in church and it's not right to scare them. We don't have altar calls because it would intimidate them."

I said, "Then you have a lot of secret Christians who are ashamed of their faith in your church, huh?" He replied, "Yes, I guess so."

I left wondering if the early church had it wrong. They were persecuted, reviled, and at times hated. Why? Because they preached Jesus Christ, crucified, buried, and raised from the dead! They were an offense to the world. If only they had heard this new gospel, they could have saved themselves from all the torment. All they had to do was to preach a lame gospel that would not have been offensive to sinners. I've heard it said, "Well, we live in a different century than the early church." Sure, a lot has happened in 2,000 years.

Whatever happened to the Scripture that says, *"Jesus Christ is the same yesterday, today, and forever"* (Heb. 13:8)? The Gospel hasn't changed! The responsibility has not changed! It is not your responsibility to save a person. It is just your responsibility to share the Gospel. Jesus said that a person only comes to the Father by the calling of the Lord (see John 6:44,65). The Word of God still does the work. It does not return void!

As I once heard said, "The church in America is gigantic, but it is only two inches deep." Who is at fault for this? Lame priests in the leadership of the church. Our feet are still shod with the preparation of the Gospel of Peace. Paul carried the gospel into many different cultures and went up against many different religions of that day. Did he preach Christ crucified to one group and another way to another group? He went into each culture with the same Jesus and the same Gospel.

He was willing to suffer whatever persecution it brought. Paul's attitude was "*...for necessity is laid upon me; yes, woe is me if I do not preach the gospel!*" (1 Cor. 9:16).

> *We are troubled on every side, yet not distressed; we are perplexed, but not in despair; persecuted, but not forsaken; cast down, but not destroyed; always bearing about in the body the dying of the Lord Jesus, that the life also of Jesus might be made manifest in our body. For we which live are always delivered unto death for Jesus' sake, that the life also of Jesus might be made manifest in our mortal flesh* (2 Corinthians 4:8-11 KJV).

This sounds like a man who is running the race, not limping along because he is lame.

What shoes are you wearing? Are they shoes of the Holy Spirit or are they created by our society? Society tells you don't make waves, don't be offensive, don't be intolerant. Be liked, be a part of the crowd, don't scare anybody with the Gospel. Stop using the name of Jesus so much; it offends people. Don't talk about the cross, the blood, hell, or judgment. Just preach love and good attitudes. That way we can have a lot of happy people who are lame Christians.

I like what Paul said, *"For I am not ashamed of the gospel of Christ; for it is the power of God unto salvation to every one that believeth; to the Jew first, and also to the Greek"* (Rom. 1:16 KJV). Rev. Steve Gallagher states in his book *Intoxicated with Babylon:*

> The Church of Jesus Christ was born in spectacular fashion; conversions were thorough and remarkable. Conditions before and after salvation were dramatically different. Converts understood that they would face persecution and possibly even death. Can you see how the people of God in the early Church lived in a definite state of separation from the unsaved around them? Those dear people would probably weep if they saw how apathetic and unseparated from the world are God's "called out ones" of today![2]

Rev. Gallagher speaks the following in *The Laodicean Church of America:*

> The first was the obvious discrepancy between Jesus's assessment of their condition and their own view of it. The Laodiceans viewed their pathetic condition in a completely positive light, oblivious of their true state. We can almost hear the abounding happiness in their voices as they boasted, "We are rich and wealthy and have need of nothing!" The unspoken inference was, "God is blessing!"

> The upbeat mindset must have been constantly reinforced through the success they were enjoying individually and as a fellowship. They probably considered their "positive mental attitude" to be faith. They were happy and things were indeed going well for them. They were not interested in "negative preaching." In the midst of their peace and prosperity the last thing they wanted to hear was a message of "gloom and doom."
>
> But Jesus told the Laodiceans something they did not know. Jesus, the Omniscient One, saw things differently. His response to their delusion was, *"You say, I am rich and have become wealthy, and have need of nothing and you do not know that you are wretched and miserable and poor and blind and naked..."* (Rev. 3:17). In His mercy He exposed them.
>
> A worldly church views success differently than Jesus views it. The former sees outward success and its trappings—large buildings, lucrative bank accounts, and hordes of idolizing followers. The latter sees the narrow path to the Cross and the inward qualities of a godly life, humility, and a real devotion to meeting the needs of others.[3]

You can substitute something so long that you don't miss the real thing: having a form of godliness and denying the true power of God in our lives.

After heart surgery I tried to eat stringently healthy. I went to the extreme of becoming a vegetarian. After about a year I found that I simply wasn't getting satisfied—I was always hungry. I found out that I wasn't getting enough protein and needed to eat more beans. Then I found a wonderful thing! I was walking through a grocery story one day, and lo and behold, I found fake meat! They made hot dogs, hamburgers, sausage, and baloney out of vegetables! It tasted pretty good! I could now have sausage for breakfast and hamburgers on the grill—it was wonderful!

After eating the meat substitute long enough I didn't miss the real thing any longer! If you are being fed a steady diet of spiritual substitutes over a long period of time you will soon forget what real meat tastes like. This dilution of spiritual truth has been so subtle it has gone undetected even by the spiritually discerning.

What do you have in your shoe? Why are you limping? Why are you lame? Put on the right shoes; get your Gospel in line with God and His holiness!

Endnotes

1. Ness, 130.

2. Steve Gallagher, *Intoxicated with Babylon* (Dry Ridge, KY: Pure Life Ministries, 2006).

3. Steve Gallagher, *The Laodicean Church of America* (Dry Ridge, KY: Pure Life Ministries), 92.

REVIEW QUESTIONS

1. What does the Bible mean when it says we must walk circumspectly?

2. What is polytheism?

3. What two main beliefs make religions different?

4. What do you feel is the world's view of today's church?

CHAPTER 5

LOOK AT THE NOSE ON THAT GUY!

"For any man who has a defect shall not approach: a man...who has a marred face...."—Leviticus 21:18

There is nothing wrong with a flat nose if that comes from a person's ancestral heritage. But the nose of a male Levite was considered perfect if it was well-rounded. Since a priest had to be born into the family, he would have a Levite nose. Why did God say that a flat nose would disqualify a priest from service?

We can look at several things that would make this blemish a disqualifying point in the ministry of a leader. Alex Ness states:

> The nose is made to house the smelling membranes. If you do not have a good smeller you will often be in deep trouble. I have saved my stomach many pains on the mission fields because of having a sensitive nose. I can smell bad food before it is brought to the table. When my nose and taste buds agree, suddenly there is no appetite.[1]

Many years ago, my father had terrible sinus problems. He was a young man and had just enlisted in the Navy to fight in the war with Japan. He had constant bad headaches. His father had been taught in his early years by an Indian to use herbal remedies to cure a number of things. My Dad went to him for help. Granddad took some dried blood root and told him to sniff it, assuring him that this would cure his sinus troubles.

My dad told me that when he sniffed the dried herb that it was like an explosion in his sinus cavities. He said he thought his head was coming off. But from that moment on he never had another sinus headache.

From that moment, however, he lost his sense of smell. We could be hiking in the woods and come across a skunk and he would never smell the animal. Once when we were walking across a field in the dark, I smelled a skunk, but Dad was ahead of me and nearly stepped on the animal and was about to be sprayed, when I yelled at him to watch out.

Dr. Ness continues his thought with:

> There are believers who can go places where they are fed pornographic filth, listen to shady stories, share cocktails, use the devil's cards and can smell no foul play. They need the Great Physician with eye salve to see and a nose to smell out that which is poisonous to the soul. As the dog that smells out narcotics, so may each New Testament priest be endowed with the "hound dog" of heaven to discern that which is unholy.

There is a further thought here pertaining to the nose. The unclean animals used their snouts to dig up unclean objects to feed upon. Swine, hedgehogs, ferrets, mice (or moles) were all pronounced unclean. They all had one thing in common: They cause destruction with their noses. They tear up the ground, stick their noses into everything possible, and fail to respect territorial rights or other people's property.

The spiritual applications become very meaningful when applied in the light of holiness. I'm talking about keeping your nose out of other people's business, not constantly searching for something to gossip about in church. The person who is a gossip is always trying to stir things up and cause discord. *"For as the churning of milk produces butter, and wringing the nose produces blood, so the forcing of wrath produces strife"* (Prov. 30:33).

The Breath in His Nostrils

I prefer this thought about the flat nose: *"And the Lord God formed man of the dust of the ground, and breathed into His nostrils the breath of life; and man became a living being"* (Gen. 2:7).

God breathed life and spirit into man's nostrils. A flat nose would imply a blockage to inspiration. If you cannot receive revelation and divine guidance from the Lord, then what do you feed those who follow you?

> *You will guide me with Your counsel, and afterward receive me to glory* (Psalm 73:24).

Inspiration is hindered by neglecting the Word of God.

One time King Saul's son, Jonathan, became separated from the rest of Israel's army. Saul was concerned about the battle and had called a fast, declaring that anyone who ate that day would be cut off from Israel. Jonathan had no knowledge of these events or the orders. He and his armor bearer were in another area.

Jonathan and his servant came upon some Philistine soldiers standing upon a hill. Jonathan and his armor bearer discussed what to do and decided to leave it in the hands of God. If the Philistines called them to come up the hill then they would accept that as God's assurance of victory. The Philistines called to them to come on up the hill. Jonathan and his armor bearer climbed the hill and fought the enemy warriors. God gave them a great victory, and when the rest of the Israelite army heard the sound of battle they joined in and defeated the Philistines that day.

On the way back, Jonathan was fatigued and hungry. He spotted a beehive in the ground and stuck his spear into it, got himself some honey, and ate. The Bible says, "*...his eyes were* ***enlightened***" (1 Sam. 14:27 KJV, emphasis added).

The Bible says the Word of God is like honey. Then we can draw the analogy that Jonathan took in the Word and was enlightened. We draw our enlightenment, our revelations, our inspiration, from the Word of the Lord.

The Spirit of God wants to move in our lives just as He did in the early church. Repeatedly we read of the Holy Spirit directing the activities of the Church. Things like, "It seems good to the Holy Spirit and us" or "the Holy Spirit said, separate Paul and Barnabas" (see Acts 15:28; 13:2). Over and over we realize that the leadership of the Church was left to the Holy Spirit who is called alongside to help us and lead us. If you cannot receive from Him, if you cannot breathe or receive from our Teacher, then you have a flat nose.

A flat nose is a hindrance in breathing in the breath of God—that which makes life and direction for a leader of the church. Did God call us to hear from Him and deliver what He has said, or to use whatever psychology, salesmanship, or speaking skills we can master? Charisma is a great asset to many people, but it still is not proof of the ability to be led by inspiration of the Holy Spirit.

> *From the ends of the earth we have heard songs: "Glory to the righteous!" But I said: "I am ruined, ruined! Woe to me!..."* (Isaiah 24:16).

What causes this spiritual leanness in the heart of a spiritual leader? I believe first is the lack of submission. This happens when we try to reason with the Lord or question everything He asks of us. Jude calls this "empty clouds" that promise rain but deliver nothing (see Jude 12). We become what we take in and what we associate ourselves with spiritually. If you are breathing in spiritual insight from God and direction from God, then you will become more godly. If you draw from a carnal life, carnal friends, or media for your inspiration, you have a flat nose and you will eventually become like them. You may cover it for a season, but eventually God will expose it. The strongest attribute in your life will rule.

I like bell peppers and my wife is a big tomato fan. So one summer I bought about seven tomato plants and put them in the back yard. Then I put in eight pepper plants—seven were bell peppers and one was a jalapeno pepper. I planted all of them beside the tomato plants and then nurtured them and watched them grow. Soon they had flowers on the plants, and after about a week small peppers began to grow on each plant.

They grew into big beautiful bell peppers, or so it appeared. When we picked them I found I had some of the largest jalapeno peppers you could harvest. All the plants were jalapeno! My first thought was a negative one. I thought for sure someone had switched the tags on the plants at the store, and I was on the receiving end. Nevertheless, we harvested the largest jalapenos I have ever seen, froze many, and gave away peppers to friends.

One day I was talking to a farmer and told him about my pepper drama. He laughed and told me that with peppers whichever species is strongest will dominate the other plants. So my one jalapeno plant was stronger and took over all of my bell pepper plants making them all into jalapeno peppers. The stronger ruled and took over the weaker strain.

Again, you can substitute something long enough that you don't recognize the real thing: having a form of godliness but denying the true power of God in our lives. These blemishes that the priests were to be free from are quite meaningless if they are not seen from the spiritual point of view. If taken literally, then a lame person or person with a flat nose could not be in ministry. At that rate, most preachers would be disqualified, for everyone has some kind of blemish. We miss the whole point if we dwell upon the physical today.

Isaiah 2:22 says, "...*breath is in his nostrils...*" and then we read where God hates the nose that is not properly proportioned. We also read that God hates the proud look, the pride of life, or pride in any form (see Isa. 3). So we could also say that God hates those with a turned-up nose! The person who says, *"Keep to yourself, do not come near me, for I am holier than you!"* (Isa. 65:5).

One such leader was Diotrephes. He is called by name only once in the Bible, in Third John 9. It is interesting to see that this was the only time we see the "apostle of love," John, writing a threatening letter. He is implying that he will use his apostolic authority in the situation involving Diotrephes. "I wrote to the church, but Diotrephes, who loves to have the preeminence among them, does not receive us." Can you imagine anyone refusing the directions of an apostle of Jesus—and not just one of the apostles but the one closest to our Lord?

The reason for Diotrophes' downfall spiritually, "He loves the preeminence," is summed up in one Greek word, *philoprooteuoon.* This is a form of *phileo* love that is performance-centered, selfish, egotistical, and prideful. He was fond of being first. Jesus talked about this when He warned of those who love the uppermost rooms at feasts and the chief seats. They loved to be greeted in the market place as Rabbi.

Diotrephes has the distinction of being the only person in the Bible about whom this word is used. It does not imply that he was doctrinally off base, but rather full of proud ambition, having the desire to promote personal authority. He refused to accept government by John. He wanted the church to be his alone without a covering from the apostle John. He was rebellious to those in authority.

John says that Diotrephes was prating against him with malicious words. The word *prating* means to "talk nonsense, to lie, to raise false accusations" (3 John 10). Malicious words are evil, wicked words. Diotrephes was content to talk about his overseer. He would not receive the brethren and he was totally against anyone who did, showing he was a very insecure man. He ruled with fear not inspiration from God. If anyone did receive the brethren he cast them out of the church. *Cast out* means "to drive, expel, send, thrust" (3 John 10).

John's warning about leaders like this is found in Third John 11: *"Beloved, do not imitate what is evil...."* Realize that Diotrophes, even though he was a leader in the New Testament Church, was classified as evil. He was not just misled or making a mistake. His attitude and love for preeminence made him apostate.

Later I will discuss remedial steps to reverse the attitudes that disqualify a person from ministry, after we have studied further God's standard of leadership.

Endnote

1. Ness, 130.

REVIEW QUESTIONS

1. Why were the swine, hedgehog, and ferret called unclean by God?

2. What hinders spiritual inspiration?

3. Who directed the activities of the early church?

4. In what ways does the same Person direct your activities?

CHAPTER 6

THE SUPERFLUOUS

"For any man who has a defect shall not approach: a man...who has...any limb too long...."—Leviticus 21:18

It was in a small country church in southern West Virginia. Nothing about the building was outstanding. It was square with white siding and a small steeple. The road ran within 12 feet of the front door. I attended a Sunday morning service there. The pastor was a hefty man in his forties, standing about 5 foot 8, and slightly balding.

He just read his text for the morning message. I noticed that he stuttered as he read. He had suffered from polio when he was a child; this caused his stutter and had caused one leg to be shorter by about 5 inches.

He wore a large built-up shoe to compensate for the short leg. After he finished his text and prayed, he began to preach. That was my first time hearing this preacher. It was not my last. The power and anointing upon his life impressed me. Under the anointing of the Spirit he soon began to pace the platform and preach eloquently, his stutter gone. It was not long until cries of "Amen" began to ring forth from that morning's crowd of listeners. The result of his sermon was an altar full of seekers.

We became close friends and worked together in meetings for several years. Physically he was superfluous, but not spiritually.

Dr. Alex Ness writes:

> The word [superfluous] means that which is disproportioned. It may be that limbs are longer one from the other. Or other parts of the body are either too large or too small. They may have two many toes or fingers, not enough or none at all. We have seen considerable amount of deformed people in Europe and America who were victims of thalidomide, or people who were victims of car accidents and are left paralyzed. Of course there is no reference that such today cannot have a ministry. These priests were spiritually representing Jesus Christ and His Church. In Jesus there was no

blemish and He is preparing a Church that is without blemish.

"That he might present it to himself a glorious church, not having spot or wrinkle, or any such thing; but that it should be holy and without blemish." (Ephesians 5:27)

The same word "superfluous" is used in Leviticus chapter 22:23 where a bullock or lamb, representing Jesus Christ must be without blemish, not superfluous or not lacking *in his parts.* In other words, the spiritual interpretation is that the type must reflect the antitype's perfection [an antitype is the fulfillment of the type].

What I see about these types is that being holy is being Christlike. Are the churches today engaged in the ministry of making men and women holy? Are leaders hungering and thirsting after righteousness as much as their own success and glory (see Matt. 5:6)? What *superfluous* speaks to us today is not the physical body, but being lopsided or imbalanced, disproportioned in our walk with Christ.

I remember being with my father when a woman came into the church asking for help for her family. She said they were living on macaroni and cheese. The only other food that the children received was at school. As she began to explain her situation to us, she explained she had an income. But she went to a church where they were taught total submission to their pastor. Anything other than submission was sin. She was chosen to pay the pastor's car payment each month, and because of this obligation to God she could not feed her children. This pastor was preaching and living a disproportional life, and because of this he was placing this woman under bondage as well as poverty.

In order not to be a superfluous leader, you must have balance in your life! Proverbs 16:11 says, *"Honest weights and scales are the Lord's; all the weights in the bag are His work."* Proverbs 20:23 states, *"Diverse weights are an abomination to the Lord, and dishonest scales are not good."* These verses and others speak of God's hatred of imbalance.

> *That we should no longer be children, tossed to and fro and carried about with every wind of doctrine, by the trickery of men, in the cunning craftiness of deceitful plotting* (Ephesians 4:14).

Webster's Dictionary defines *balance* as "a counterweight on the opposite side of a scale to produce equilibrium or steadiness; to render equal in proportion; to adjust." My wife Karren enjoys watching gymnastics during the Olympics. We are always amazed watching the young girls on the balance beam. It is amazing how they have learned to do twists and flips while balancing themselves on that narrow wooden beam. One misstep and the gymnast's balance is off and she falls to the floor.

Ephesians 3:17-21 says, *"[I pray] that you, being rooted and grounded in love, may be able to comprehend with all the saints what is the width and length and depth and height—to know the love of*

Christ...." The depth of Christ's love is not limited to someone's box, their ideal, their theology. People have a tendency to box in their concepts.

Balance in the Christian life consists of continually learning and growing in a relationship with the Lord Jesus Christ. He is our balance. God wants to reveal Himself to each of His children. No father wants to know his son by proxy through another child. God is the same. He doesn't want to know His spiritual children by relaying His message secondhand through others. However He may not reveal himself in the same way or at the same time to each person.

When God is revealing one particular facet of Himself we may mistake this revelation as imbalance. An example is that He may want to reveal Himself as Baptizer in the Holy Spirit, focusing a person's attention entirely on that one aspect of Himself, until they respond by accepting. In the meantime that person is consumed with one thing. They see it everywhere, they read it in everything, they hear it everywhere, until it is learned. The area of truth can become more to them than the Truth Himself. You can gather around truth and then become exclusive. You have it and no one else does. Then the basis of fellowship is that you agree to doctrine or to the leader's ideas.

Imbalance comes if we attempt to separate from the person of Jesus Christ what is in fact a part of His personality, character, or way—if we choose to glorify an aspect of Christ, instead of Christ Himself.

Jesus is the Healer, Jesus is the Deliver, Jesus is the Provider, Jesus is the Teacher, Jesus is the Evangelist, Jesus is the Baptizer. Faith comes from Him, prosperity comes by Him!

When you find you are depending on experiences, techniques, rules, or ritual rather than your personal relationship with God, you are in danger of becoming imbalanced. We must always strive to stay centered in Jesus and all that He is.

There are many aspects of this faith in Christ, and all of them can be carried to the extreme at the expense of the others. These aspects include: authority, gifts, prosperity, suffering, sacrifice, holiness, deliverance, evangelism, love, correction, discipline, etc. *"Be not righteous over much; neither make thyself over wise: why shouldest thou destroy thyself? Be not over much wicked, neither be thou foolish: why shouldest thou die before thy time?"* (Eccl. 7:16-17 KJV). The New International Version translates verse 18, *"...The man who fears God will avoid all extremes."*

These texts are speaking of self-righteousness and show us that the God-fearing person will avoid both extremes (legalism and libertinism) and lead a balanced righteous life. Extremism usually takes on a form known as self-righteousness or sanctimoniousness.

The Corinthian church is a good example of those who got into misusing their gifts and authority. Even to the extreme of self-righteousness, claiming one was better than the other, because of the individual who baptized them. Then the apostle Paul wrote to help get them back on track.

Today we have those who go to the extreme on emotionalism and those who go to the opposite direction and are completely stoic. The very first revival I ever conducted was at a church where everything was connected to the emotional. If everyone wasn't slain in the spirit in every service then you didn't really have a church service.

There are two extremes in emotionalism. There are two extremes in holiness. There are two extremes in submission and there are two extremes in prosperity. For many years the church believed in keeping the minister poor because that was a sign of holiness. The message was, "Keep him on his knees seeking God."

Truths can be paradoxical. Just like a quarter, one side has an eagle and the other side a face. You can view the picture side and neglect the eagle side. You can preach prosperity and neglect suffering or preach suffering and neglect prosperity—and then judge the one who preaches the opposite truth.

All the spokes on a bike tire must be the same size or the tire becomes imbalanced. The tires on your car must be balanced for a smooth ride, otherwise the front end of your vehicle begins to shake and eventually you cannot continue. The same is true of your life.

Paul says in First Corinthians 9:25 that we must be temperate (balanced) in all things. I remember hearing the story of five blind men who were taken to an elephant and asked to describe what they felt. One man put his hand on the leg and said, "It's a stump." One man at the tail said, "No, it's a rope." The man by the ears said, "It's a fan." The man by the trunk said, "It's a hose." And the one in the middle said, "It's a wall." Each one's opinion seemed to be contradictory until further knowledge was revealed.

The idea is, don't let new knowledge get out of balance. Once you receive one side, wait on the other. After knowledge comes balance!

> *But also for this very reason, giving all diligence, add to your faith virtue, to virtue knowledge, to knowledge self-control, to self-control perseverance, to perseverance godliness, to godliness brotherly kindness, and to brotherly kindness love* (2 Peter 1:5-7).

The superfluous leader becomes preoccupied with just one part of truth. Leaders need to lead like Acts 20:27 describes, *"For I have not shunned to declare to you the* ***whole counsel*** *of God"* (emphasis mine).

Being lopsided does not mean that you are preaching falsehood. It means you may be taking one truth in Christ to the extreme, while neglecting the fullness of the Gospel of Christ. These areas of imbalance may not disqualify a leader, but can create discord, confusion, and bondage in the Body of Christ.

Another area of imbalance is when a Christian leader tries to balance ministry and sinful behavior. The question raised is: Can a man or woman of God, who should be striving for righteousness and holiness in his or her life, serve alcohol and God at the same time? I have talked to men who have told me that they have gotten into the pulpit to preach on a Sunday night drunk. Then there are some who try to balance the pulpit while having an affair with someone in the congregation, who skim the offering plate while preaching the love of Christ, or who preach tithing while they themselves don't practice tithing.

Anyone would recognize that living one life in the pulpit and another at home is sin. It is presumption and hypocrisy. Another such example today is men and women who continue on in the priestly profession while they are hooked on pornography. John tells us, *"If we say that we have fellowship with Him, and walk in darkness, we lie and do not practice the truth"* (1 John 1:6). You cannot say it any plainer than that.

I am not saying they have no hope! Repentance is always an open door to those who seek it. The apostle John continues in verses 8-9:

> *If we say that we have no sin, we deceive ourselves, and the truth is not in us. If we confess our sins, He is faithful and just to forgive us our sins and to cleanse us from all unrighteousness.*

Thank God, he said ***all*** unrighteousness, not just some. Holiness is still being Christlike!

REVIEW QUESTIONS

1. Are there areas in your life that are imbalanced?

2. What is balance in a believer's life?

3. Where does imbalance come from?

4. Being lopsided does not mean you are preaching falsehood. What does it mean?

Chapter 7

THE BROKEN-FOOTED

"For any man who has a defect shall not approach: . . . a man who has a broken foot. . . ."—Leviticus 21:18-19

As my wife Karren was leaving to speak at a women's conference, she asked me to check the pool's vacuum to see if it was working properly. After determining that the vacuum was working as it should, I stepped off the pool deck onto the stairs and the stairs gave way, sending me sprawling and breaking my fibula. The doctor set my ankle in a cast and sent me home. I was now temporarily broken-footed!

This created several problems. I couldn't stand or walk without crutches, my suit slacks would not fit over the cast, and I could not drive my car. I started wearing crazy wear from the gym because it would stretch over the cast. A few days later I received a call from a church about 350 miles from my home. They wanted me to come for a week of services. I informed the pastor that I couldn't drive and I couldn't wear my suits. I would have to preach while wearing sweatpants and with the aid of crutches. They would also have to send a driver to chauffer me there. He called me back a day later and said they had a driver and wanted me to come with my handicaps.

I preached and prayed for people at the altar, while I held onto a crutch and wore my sweatpants. God didn't seem to mind. The anointing was strong and the crowds seemed to be a little bigger. (I think people came to see the strangely dressed preacher.)

The Old Testament type shows us that a priest could not show a perfect Christ if he had to use a crutch. He could not hold the sacrifice, do the heave offering, or conduct most of his priestly duties. Likewise with me, I had to depend on others, change my attire, and hobble on crutches. Alex Ness states in chapter six, page 133 of his book, *Holiness:*

> A broken footed man must use crutches or some artificial means of support. He cannot walk properly without some outside help. Do you recognize this problem in yourself or others? You may say I just cannot keep going without that shot of cocaine or a beer. I must have that cigarette or puff of marijuana. What is it that you must use to prop you up? Are you dependant upon

> an outside prop to hold you up, or are your steps ordered of the Lord and your walk firm and of a sure step on the narrow way?[1]

"Then you will walk safely in your way, and your foot will not stumble" (Prov. 3:23). Humankind was made to have dominion over all things, and all things shall be under our feet. *"Thou madest him to have dominion over the works of Thy hands; Thou hast put all things under his feet"* (Ps. 8:6 KJV). *"For He hath put all things under His feet. But when He saith all things are put under Him, it is manifest that He is excepted, which did put all things under Him"* (1 Cor. 15:27 KJV). *"And hath put all things under His feet, and gave Him to be the head over all things to the church"* (Eph. 1:22 KJV).

The Church must not have limp, useless, broken feet but be able to stand in warfare.

> *Stand therefore, having your loins girt about with truth, and having on the breastplate of righteousness; and your feet shod with the preparation of the gospel of peace* (Ephesians 6:14-15 KJV).

We have been given the authority and power to tread on satan and his demonic powers.

> *Behold, I give unto you power to tread on serpents and scorpions, and over all the power of the enemy; and nothing shall by any means hurt you* (Luke 10:19 KJV).

As I explained in my first book, *Attitudes of Great Leaders,* the feet represent authority. When a leader misuses authority or is hypocritical with authority, he is broken-footed.

Just this week the governor of my state resigned his position. Here was a man given authority by the people of the state to govern their lives and enforce their laws. He was known as a governor who was tough on prostitution rings and had prosecuted several. Then he was exposed for patronizing a prostitution ring for years while enforcing the laws upon the others. This incident is an example of hypocrisy and of misuse of the authority delegated to him.

The problem is that this is not unique. I could share about congressmen, senators, governors, and even presidents—men and women who have let position and power overcome them and then think that they are immune. But it doesn't stop there. It also slinks into our church leaders and pastors, preaching against sins such as pornography, adultery, and homosexuality, while secretly engaging in these same sins. The question is not, "Is this sin?" The question is, "When does God disqualify someone?" Certainly long before their constituents or congregations realize God has lifted His anointing. Eventually God brings everything to light. All those things that are hidden are exposed.

> *For it is shameful even to speak of those things which are done by them in secret. But all things that are exposed are made manifest by the light, for whatever makes manifest is*

> *light. Therefore He says: "Awake, you who sleep, arise from the dead, and Christ will give you light." See then that you walk circumspectly, not as fools but as wise, redeeming the time, because the days are evil* (Ephesians 5:12-16).

> *In this the children of God and the children of the devil are manifest: Whoever does not practice righteousness is not of God, nor is he who does not love his brother* (1 John 3:10).

When is enough, enough with God? I don't know where God draws the line with someone who repeatedly returns to the same sin while professing the opposite. If you are broken-footed, that means you cannot walk circumspectly as God commands. You are using something else to prop you up. What is your crutch? Sometimes the crutch can be your mind. You can convince yourself that you are exempt from a blemished spirit, or that God understands your sinful desires or faults.

A man or woman of God must have his or her feet shod with the Gospel of Peace. You must be able to walk in the Word. Step back and take a look. Evaluate yourself! How much time do you spend in prayer? How much time do you take reading your Bible? Is it really that simple? I believe it all comes down to our relationship with our Father. You need prayer to communicate with Him. You need the Word of God to communicate with you.

Is the Word in your heart or merely in your brain? Have you meditated upon it enough to change your life and create inspiration?

I once heard a message about the four principles of learning. First is the mind; we need to *memorize*. Then comes *meditation*, which is the incubation of the Word—like placing an egg into an incubator and waiting. As that egg is incubated, it turns into something new. Soon you have a chick hatched. As you meditate on the Word of God it is incubated and soon moves to your heart where it becomes *inspiration*. Finally inspiration can become *revelation* that you can walk in and see manifest in your life.

Our authority comes through a relationship with the one who delegates His authority to us!

Paul told Titus, "*These things speak, and exhort, and rebuke with all authority. Let no man despise thee*" (Titus 2:15 KJV). Paul speaks expressly to Titus and gives him a charge. Then he tells him, "Let no man despise you. Don't let anyone back you into a corner. Don't feel uncomfortable because you had to rebuke someone. You are doing it under God's authority."

The word used in the Greek here for authority is *epitage*. This word is used interchangeably with the English word *power*. It means "to decree by authoritativeness." Paul possesses authority and he gives the authority he possesses to his protégé.

Before we can tell someone to follow this authority, it has to be personal first. We need to be closely knit with authority; we need to be familiar with authority; we need to be associated with authority.

In Matthew 11, two disciples of John come to Jesus and asked Him if He is the one they are looking for. Jesus doesn't respond with, "I'm born of a virgin," or quote 40 generations of His lineage, or tell them, "I'm the Son of David and the Son of Abraham." He says, "Go tell John what you hear and see." He could have rattled off a résumé but He said, "Go tell John what you heard and saw." What was that? The blind see, the lame walk, the Gospel is preached to the poor.

The last thing Jesus said is what most preachers promote first. Their great oratory skills, the ability to articulate a thought in a fantastic way, dramatics and theatrics. The last thing Jesus mentioned was preaching to the poor. We give credit to lip service and we miss the fact that authentic ministry is twofold: what you hear and what you see!

In Acts chapter 4 we see men who are shifted from discipleship to believership! A disciple is a learner who will eventually graduate to operating under his own faith in what he has been taught. At that point he has shifted to the authority of a believer instead of the authority of a disciple. In Acts 4 Peter and John are now into believership. They are now walking in authority. Guess who gets upset? The religious people. Their question was, "Who gives you this power and authority?" (see Acts 4:7).

Peter could say here, "My Savior has gone on to the other side; you crucified Him. But I can show He is real. This healed man vouches for the Jesus Christ who is not here in person." The priest took note that these were unlearned and ignorant men, unqualified according to their standards. Their expertise was they had been with Jesus!

My authority doesn't come from my history, my culture, my affiliation, my organizational ties, or from my social connections. It comes from my relationship with Jesus! Authority does not come from a bookshelf. You and I need to have proof and examples that God is in fact backing up our lives with authority.

Relationships keep you from being broken-footed.

If what you have is based upon the Word totally, it cannot be questioned. You need to be recognized as someone who has been in the presence of the Lord. You cannot walk in authority just because of your position or title. Your authority is going to be established by proof and by people's perception of whose presence you have been in before you came to that pulpit or place of leadership.

When a pastor walks to the pulpit he or she doesn't have to walk around with a sign on his back saying, *I'm a pastor*. When you walk into a room people will feel the presence of God and recognize, "That's a man or woman of God."

I had this experience in an Arby's restaurant. I was going there for lunch pretty regularly because I liked a chicken sandwich they served. The manager happened to be working the register that day. After taking my order, she asked, "Can I ask you a question?"

"Sure," I said. Then she said, "No, I better not ask. You might get angry." "No, no, go ahead. Ask. I won't get mad." Besides I was really curious by now. She asked me, "Are you a pastor?" My jeans and tennis shoes certainly didn't look pastoral. I asked her, "What made you ask that question?" She said, "I've seen you every day you've come in and there is just something different about you from the rest of the people in line."

People ought to be able to discern you have been with Jesus.

In Acts 8:19 we see the word *epitage* when Simon the sorcerer is asking Peter to sell him his authority. The key here is that Simon the sorcerer had been accustomed to using tricks and gimmicks for influence, but he knew he had no real spiritual authority. He knew that he was not acquainted with the kind of power the apostles had. He thought authority could be purchased! However it is not for sale. It cannot be purchased.

This kind of authority does not come with human attachment. This kind of authority comes from a relationship with God; outside of that relationship there is no true authority.

Ministry right now is being manipulated into who can get the best video or best picture, or market most effectively. Public relations firms are now in great demand by preachers. There are folks out there who are fixing people up to be stars in ministry. They think, "If I can get into the right arena, it will give me authority."

Like Simon, you cannot buy the influence of God for your own personal gain. Authority is coming out of hypocrisy into relationship with God. We must always maintain our submission to the One who delegates our position and power to us.

We have to understand how important authentic leadership is. We have to know how important anointed leadership is. We have to be the kind of leader who is in touch with Heaven.

Be the kind of leader who hears from God! Be the kind of leader who hears God's voice over the voice of the people. Be the kind of leader who delivers people in times of trouble. Be the kind of leader who can get the people ready for the return of Jesus! Be the kind of leader who walks and carries himself or herself the same way in the church and outside the church.

You cannot lead that way if you have broken feet. Be a leader of integrity. Resist the devil and he will flee from you!

Endnote

1. Ness, 133.

REVIEW QUESTIONS

1. When do you think enough is enough with God?

2. Have you meditated on the Word enough to change your life? In what way?

3. What are the four principles of learning mentioned in this chapter?

4. What kind of leader hears from God?

CHAPTER 8

THE BROKEN-HANDED

"For any man who has a defect shall not approach: a man...who has a...broken hand...."—Leviticus 21:18-19

Imagine a man named Thomas who lived in Israel during Old Testament days. Having known the law forbade any blemish on a sacrificial animal, Thomas had searched diligently for the perfect sheep. He had made the earliest available appointment with the Levite priests a month prior. Thomas had marveled aloud to his wife at how busy the Levites must be. Now, one month later, the day had come.

The searing Israeli sun pounded relentlessly on Thomas's and his 12-year-old son's shoulders as they led their unwitting, unblemished sacrificial lamb through the busy, dusty streets of Israel. As he approached the gates to the tabernacle, Thomas was surprised not to see John, his long-time priest and friend.

"Where's John?"

"I'm terribly sorry, Thomas. He's taken a bad fall and broken his hand. He won't be allowed to touch a sacrifice with a broken hand. Nor will he be able to perform the heave offering. My name is Levi. I will serve as your priest."

Hands are important in the Bible. There are 1,470 references to the *hand* and 527 more for *hands*. Hands signify work, labor, ability, ownership, blessing, and the means of spiritual transference:

> 1 Timothy 5:22: *Lay hands suddenly on no man, neither be partaker of other men's sins: keep thyself pure* (KJV).
>
> Mark 5:23: *And besought Him greatly, saying, My little daughter lieth at the point of death: I pray thee, come and lay thy hands on her, that she may be healed; and she shall live* (KJV).
>
> Mark 6:2: *And when the sabbath day was come, He began to teach in the synagogue: and many hearing Him were astonished, saying, From whence hath this Man these things? and what wisdom is this which is given unto Him, that even such mighty works are wrought by His hands?* (KJV).

The Bible even speaks of the doctrine of laying on of hands in Hebrews 6:2: *"Of the doctrine of baptisms, and* ***of laying on of***

hands, *and of resurrection of the dead, and of eternal judgment"* (KJV, emphasis added).

Dr. Ness states in his book *Holiness.*

> A man with a broken hand is just as handicapped as the one with a broken foot. Their number is legion in our midst. They are forever complaining about their aches and pains, never able to give a lifting hand because their hand is broken. They cannot give anyone a good hearty Christian handshake because their hand is broken. I have shaken hands with tens of thousands in every continent of the world. Some were bone crushers and some were the faint type that you wondered if you had hold of a marshmallow. Some were stiff as a mannequin, others slippery as a fish. But there is that firm yet gentle, look in the eye with sincerity genuine one that you know their hand is neither deformed nor broken.
>
> God's priest cannot serve Him properly with spiritually broken hands. They may see the wounded in the ditch but unlike the Samaritan, they cannot lift the wounded onto their beast. They cannot earn their own living much less provide for others. Their hand is too sore to reach into their pocketbook to pay their tithes and too crippled to write an encouraging letter.

They cannot lift up holy hands to the Lord in worship.

I remember receiving a résumé from a minister looking for a church to pastor in the district I was overseeing. He had been in ministry for nine years. During those nine years he had served nine different churches as pastor, one year each. He evidently felt that this was a wonderful accomplishment. What I saw was a man who could not deal with conflict, could not minister to his congregation, and constantly ran from his problems. He had evidently served each church until the honeymoon season was over and the problems began. Proverbs 10:4 says, *"He who has a slack hand becomes poor, but the hand of the diligent makes rich."*

I have seen men take churches of 100 or more, then several years later leave them with 8 or 10 people—feeling it was time to move on to greener pastures. Why? Because their hand was broken and they could not minister spiritually to the needs of their congregations. You cannot counsel, minister, or discipline those in the Body who have need, if you yourself are burnt out or depleted. We must be ready to give that hand, or lay that hand on the broken and downcast. If you yourself are that broken and downcast, then you are broken-handed.

It is important to understand the stages of our Christian experience. They can recycle many times in our Christian walk—especially as leaders! Taking time to heal is important.

One thing to remember is that we change in our Christian experience. But God never changes! I like to call the first stage of our Christian experience the *Dynamic Stage*. This phase in your life is when you are hungry and thirsty for the things of God, on fire for Jesus, in communion with Jesus, and the fire of the Holy Spirit is burning in you. You are rejoicing in the Lord! You want to believe God's Word. You cry out, "God give me a mountain to move!" God says He will heal, and you believe it. God says He will save and you believe it. God says He will supply your needs and you believe it. You cannot get enough of church, you cannot get enough of the Word. You are constantly hungry for more of God. This is the first stage of salvation! God wants you to live in this stage. This stage can come back time and time again. It ceases when we are no longer living where we are really trusting Him alone.

Then there is the *Deteriorating Stage*. The love and joy and peace and excitement for Jesus begins to fade away. There are two kinds of people here: there are those who are in a static time, struggling to believe God for something for so long. When they finally receive it, their faith is growing, until they sit back and say, "I can relax now. I've been filled with the Holy Ghost for years now; I can lay hands on the sick; I can cast out devils." After so long they feel like they have done their part and want to settle down.

Then there are those whose faith hasn't worked. So they talk themselves into a lesser walk. They seek the safety that inaction offers. They begin to excuse why they are not on fire. They begin to justify themselves. It's my wife, it's my husband, the board didn't give me a chance. Sin will rust through in their spiritual lives.

I remember reading the story of how an Indian tribe would determine their princess. They chose certain young women and then sent them into a cornfield. The women were instructed to pick the largest ear of corn in their row. The girl with the largest ear of corn would become the princess. The young women would walk through the row of corn and look for the largest ear. However, they were forbidden to go back for an ear once they had passed it. Many would come to the end with empty hands because they were always looking for a larger ear up ahead.

During this stage we justify our failures or we deny their reality. We pass the buck and blame some minister, our job, or traditions. Satan wants to destroy your zeal. You need to know this stage. If you are not in the Dynamic Stage and you have not fallen, then you may be glancing in that direction.

The third stage is the *Dry Stage,* where we have left our first love, as it says in Revelation 2:4. If you are a preacher in this stage, you step into the pulpit and the buzz is gone. You feel like the school bus driver that loves to drive the bus, but hates all the kids he has to pick up. In the first stage you can't get enough of Jesus, revivals, or church. But in the Dry Stage you begin to be too busy to study or pray. In the Dynamic Stage you always had time for God, always scheduled God in daily. Now you're just too busy.

Satan is no fool. He works a little at a time to get you sidetracked. He divides your attention. Soon your temper gets away from you. Whereas before you would repent, now you excuse it.

It's hard to believe that a spiritual leader can slip into the Dry Stage, but it happens every day. There are many important godly things that start to occupy your time. I remember one pastor who had a growing church, a Christian school, a Christian bookstore, and a college. All of these demanded his time, in addition to the normal pastoral duties. He was not one who delegated, so he tried to stay on top of all these responsibilities himself. He shared with me once that the only time he had to read his Bible was as he drove, resting the Bible on his steering wheel. The sad end of this story is that he became dry and tried to work under his own power. He eventually had an affair and fell away from the ministry.

It's difficult to fathom any of us slipping from the dynamic phase and not realizing something is wrong. It's like driving down the road and your car begins to wobble. Do you recognize that something is wrong? If your oil light comes on and you place some duct tape over the light, does that fix the problem? Or does it just help you ignore it until it is too late?

If you are driving down life's journey, enjoying the things of God and deterioration sets in, you begin to become flat and you don't have enough sense to change the tire. You are headed for a crash. Better start reading your Bible!

The *Discovery Stage* is the stage when we wake up and discover our spiritual condition. It's a time for real honesty with yourself—when you come to a realization that you cannot do this without Him. In this stage you discover that you are dry and it's not someone else's fault. Learn the symptoms of a broken hand. When the peace, the joy, and the stirring isn't there anymore, acknowledge that something is wrong.

The *Delightful Stage* is the stage where you know the certainties of His love, faith, and longsuffering again. When you say, "I'm not going back one inch," you no are longer going to be deceived or allow yourself to deteriorate again. You fight for your joy, you fight for victory, you resist the devil.

I once got into a conflict with my father, who was a senior minister, and I became deeply wounded by his words and actions. I tried to convince myself his attitude was because of his health and the medical condition that he was battling at the time. But because we were so close, I found myself wounded in my spirit. It seemed that all I could do was weep. It left me totally drained spiritually and emotionally. I was pastoring at the time and found myself unable to minister to others. I felt so dead and dry inside, depleted of all spiritual joy and zeal. I could have put on a face and continued on in my natural abilities, but that would not have been fair to the church. There was really nothing I could give from my empty well.

I went to the elders of the church and explained to them that I was burned out spiritually and needed a break to restore myself. They understood and consented to divide my responsibilities between themselves. I was asked to make sure I was in all the services where I could be fed spiritually with the

Word and ministry. I was broken-handed and needed time to heal and be ministered to.

Being a pastor or Christian leader is not all about talent, looks, education, or charisma. It is about being full of the spirit. It's about being able to feed your people with spiritual food and ministering to their spiritual needs. This requires us to be full of the Spirit as the Word commands. If not then you are broken-handed.

REVIEW QUESTIONS

1. What do hands signify in the Bible?

2. After reading the section on stages of the Christian experience, what stage do you think you are currently in?

3. What do you think a leader should do when he finds himself burned out?

Chapter 9

THE CROOK-BACKED

"For any man who has a defect shall not approach: ...a hunchback...."—Leviticus 21:18,20

It's the Sabbath and Jesus is teaching in the synagogue, when a woman enters to worship. This woman doesn't look up but makes her way toward a seating area. She walks with a bent-over shuffle, her spine racked by disease. The effort of looking up or even lifting her arms above her head requires strenuous effort. Jesus is teaching a lesson illustrated by a story about a gardener and a fig tree, yet He sees her enter and watches her hobble to her seat. The Bible says that she had a spirit of infirmity for eighteen years, and was bent over, and could in no way lift herself up (see Luke 13:11-13).

Jesus stops teaching and calls her over to Him. Everyone watches to see what He will do. He lays His hands on her and says, "Woman, you are loosed from your infirmity." Immediately she is made straight. She begins leaping and jumping! She shouts and gives glory to God!

The ruler of the synagogue is indignant because Jesus has healed this woman on the Sabbath day. The answer that Jesus gives in Luke 13:16 shows us that this blemish of being crook-backed is caused by satan. The Bible also says that it was caused by a spirit of infirmity. Jesus also lets us know that she was *"a daughter of Abraham,"* in the same gracious sense, no doubt, as Zaccheus after his conversion was *"a son of Abraham"* (Luke 19:9).

Being bent over or bound, having a racked spine, would be a great infirmity to deal with. In his book *Holiness,* Dr. Ness states:

> When the back has become crooked, the whole body begins to stoop. The head is bent low to the earth and takes a form for which man was not created. When you are stooped you cannot look man in the eyes or lift your face and eyes to the heavens.
>
> A crookbacked priest could neither portray the Lord or the Church. For even the Church is referred to as *"This thy stature is like a palm tree."* (Song of Solomon 7:7), and that she is altogether perfect.
>
> The priest had to be perfect physically. A crooked back would be a very evident blemish. He could not effectively

> offer the sacrifice, heave the offering or raise his arms to bless the people.
>
> Neither can a crook represent the Lord. There are those who have placed themselves into the ministry. They are in submission to no one, give an account to no one for their ministry, talents or finances. They operate crookedly; they live crooked lives and bring disgrace to the cause of God.[1]

We know that the Old Testament type is an illustration of a person being unable to show the perfection of Christ. Being crook-backed disqualified a man from becoming a priest—he was not representative of the biblical type.

One of the areas of strength in a man is his back. While in Army basic training we were told to fill sandbags with fresh sand, carry them to our barracks, and pour the sand on the ground around the barracks area. (Evidently the drill sergeant felt that the area wasn't sandy enough.) So all day we filled bags with sand, carried them nearly four blocks, and poured the sand on the ground. Over and over again we would hear the drill sergeant say, "Come on ladies, put your backs into it!"

Nehemiah 8:10 says, *"...The joy of the lord is your strength"!* We sing the song "The Joy of the Lord Is My Strength!" This song is taken from the text in Nehemiah, but the preceding verses, Nehemiah 8:1-10, tell us how to obtain and maintain the joy of the Lord.

At the time that these words were proclaimed, the Israelites had just returned from captivity in Babylon. Under the leadership of Ezra and Nehemiah, Israel had rebuilt the ruined walls and the temple and was restoring the nation. At this point Nehemiah called a special meeting at the city's water gate. Nehemiah 8:1 says, *"All the people gathered together as one man...."* The first thing you have to do is make yourself available to God. There were 42,360 Israeli men, not including the women, and 7,300 servants, which included 245 singers. That's over 50,000 people who were gathered to hear the Word of God! The Bible says that the people were hungry to hear the Word and they were attentive. They were fully prepared to submit to the authority of God's Word.

The next statement is amazing. Ezra preached to this crowd for hours, from morning to midday, yet no one noticed the time! The ears of all the people were attentive unto the book of the law.

Can you imagine? All these people were captivated by God's Word! The next question is: Can you imagine this in the churches of today? Here we see the true source of revival and joy: a love for the Word of God. True strength of spirit and leadership come from a hunger for the Word and relationship with the Father.

At times Ezra was so overcome by what he read, he stopped to "bless the Lord the Great God!" Then the Glory of the Lord came down powerfully, and all the people raised their hands in praise to God. They humbled themselves before God in brokenness and repentance at the pure Word of God!

A half-day of preaching wasn't enough for these hungry people. For the remainder of the day they formed groups, with 17 elders leading them in Bible studies. The Word of God caused the people to understand their sin! Can you picture this scene? Fifty thousand people lying scattered on the ground, face down, mourning for their sin in unison.

What is God's testimony? God's testimony is never that His people are lying on their faces, crying rivers of tears. The testimony He wants to bring forth in His leaders and people is joy—genuine, lasting joy. "The joy of the Lord is your strength!" Joy that results from biblical study and true repentance brings true strength to God's people. Repentance is the mother of all joy in Jesus!

King David sinned and disobeyed God. He lost the joy of the Lord, and that joy could not be restored except by true repentance. He grew week and discouraged, so he prayed, *"Wash me thoroughly from my iniquity, and cleanse me from my sin, restore unto me the joy of my salvation"* (see Ps. 51:7-12).

In Nehemiah 8:9-10 Ezra told the crowds, "You've been excited about God's Word, hungering for it, loving it, allowing it to work in your hearts. You have repented, wept, and mourned and God is pleased with you. But now it's time to rejoice. Take out your handkerchiefs and wipe away your tears. This is a time of great joy and mirth." They spent the next seven days rejoicing. What a party!

To have strength in your life, you must have the Word of God in your life continually, and you must be humble enough to repent of your sins.

We could give many reasons for a lack of strength and the inability to put your back into the work, but one main reason is because your heart is just not in the work.

> *Amaziah was twenty and five years old when he began to reign, and he reigned twenty and nine years in Jerusalem. And his mother's name was Jehoaddan of Jerusalem. And he did that which was right in the sight of the Lord, but not with a perfect heart* (2 Chronicles 25:1-2 KJV).

King Amaziah started out pretty well. Whether he did what was right out of habit or necessity we don't know, but we do know that his heart wasn't in serving God. He worshiped the God of Israel. He made sure that the temple worship was taking place. But he was not a man of devotion himself.

I believe we see a lot of this doing what is good, but without the heart being right in this Church age. Jesus said of this kind of Christianity: *"Behold, I stand at the door and knock. If anyone hears My voice and opens the door, I will come in to him and dine with him, and he with Me"* (Rev. 3:20). He is talking to a church that is full of people, rich monetarily, and has many great programs. Everything the world counts as success and good marketing, but one thing is missing—Jesus!

Amaziah did things right in the eyes of the Lord, but not with a pure heart. He brought into his house idols from other nations to worship. How many people are serving God and keeping secret sins at home? They are crook-backed, no strength in them. They have an inability to worship and lift up their eyes and hands in worship to our Christ. You cannot worship to your fullest potential when you are bent over by your sins.

Amaziah became rebellious or crook-backed. God sent a prophet to tell him that he didn't approve of his secret sin of idol worship. He refused the counsel of God and threatened the prophet. Some men and women in ministry feel above repentance. They think that they are exempt because God has made them special. They will say, "God understands my need and my personality."

I remember one pastor who once shared with my father that women were always hitting on him and that one woman had come to him and told him that she could not live without a man. Later in life my father confronted him with evidence of adultery. He denied all accounts and continued on as pastor of the church. Years later, after his funeral, a woman came forward and admitted having an affair with this pastor for over 25 years.

Just think, this pastor had stepped into the pulpit every Sunday for all those years and declared the Word of the Lord while his heart was not perfect with the Lord. He had convinced himself that he was OK because God understood his need and because this poor woman could not live without a man. Self-delusion is a major cause of becoming crook-backed.

I had a talk with a brother once who had been missing a lot of church services. He told me he was going undercover buying cocaine and wearing a wire for the police. I asked him how he could do this knowing that he had to use drugs himself in order to prove his sincerity to the pushers. He said to me, "Pastor, God has told me that I am different. God said that I cannot get addicted."

Today he is serving a 20-year sentence for drug possession and sales. Why? Because he allowed himself to lose his way by self-delusion. No one is above temptation or sin.

Sometimes we get bent over by the weight of our job. We have no joy because our heart isn't in the work or because we are trying to be someone else or please someone else.

In First Samuel 17, King Saul tried to get David to wear his armor to fight Goliath. David had trouble walking in the heavy armor and told the king, "No thanks!"

David already had his ministry and style. He had learned it watching sheep and fellowshipping with God. He was not completely unlearned in war because he had been Saul's armor bearer prior to coming forward to fight Goliath.

Have you ever wished your ministry was like someone else's? I have admired men of God who could preach with great zeal and a powerful anointing. But we need to recognize that leaders come in many different varieties, shapes, and forms. You cannot generalize the role of ministering for the Lord. You get trapped when you try to live up to other people's expectations—that can be overwhelming.

The Bible says that Saul was head and shoulders over everyone. That means he was the tallest man in Israel. Here is poor young David in front of the king, and he is told to wear the king's armor. Several things were wrong with this: The armor wasn't designed to fit David, it wasn't comfortable for his way of fighting, and he didn't have a hope of victory wearing it. In the same way, you cannot wear another person's ministry. The armor is not designed for you. God created each one of us to be different. We must learn to be content with who we are.

What causes us to falter this way? Our insecurities such as inferiority, fear of rejection, or judgmental spirits. All of these can cause you to lose heart in your ministry. Sometimes a judgmental spirit doesn't say anything. You merely sense you are being judged. This spirit can rob you of confidence, and even cause you to doubt your calling and anointing. It cries, "Your armor is not like mine! It won't work as well as mine!"

One Sunday-school teacher was excited over the fruit of his class. He looked forward all week long to opening the Word and feeling the anointing while he taught. Then a couple started attending the church. The wife announced she had taught the Bible for years and had quite a reputation. She said,

"I'm interested in what insights you might have. I'm going to sit in on your class." This caused instant intimidation in the current adult teacher.

The following four or five Sundays, she sat in the front row with her notebook and pencil. She also purchased the tape of every lesson, and at the close of the class she would come up and offer suggestions of improvement.

After a while the teacher found himself automatically looking in her direction to see how his statements were received. Soon the joy was gone. Sunday mornings were dreaded. Heaviness replaced joy, all from that judgmental spirit. Week after week, she was really saying, "Here, wear my armor—it's better. Do it my way." That judgmental spirit attacks your insecurity and your calling!

Be like David. He knew his call! He refused to be intimidated. He knew what God had anointed in his life. He said, "I'm using my staff and sling. I will be who I am!" Don't let your strength be sapped away. Don't become crook-backed.

Endnote

1 Ness, 136.

REVIEW QUESTIONS

1. What does this chapter say is the true source of revival and joy?

2. Have you lost the joy in your experience? If so what does this chapter teach you about restoring it?

3. What did King David do to restore his joy?

4. Can you do things correctly but with a wrong heart?

5. Have you ever been intimidated in ministry by someone? How did you deal with it?

Chapter 10

THE SPIRITUALLY SMALL

"For any man who has a defect shall not approach: ...a dwarf...."—Leviticus 21:18,20

Just imagine a day at the temple in Israel several thousand years ago. You are standing in the courtyard holding onto your sacrificial bull, waiting on a priest to take your offering to the Lord.

Out of the temple comes a priest. He is a bit unusual and you stare in amazement. He is less than 4 feet tall and very slim and sickly. He walks toward you and takes the bullock by the halter and tries to lead him to the altar. The bullock shies away; perhaps it smells the others that have died. The animal starts to drag the small priest across the courtyard. You think to yourself, *This would be funny if it wasn't such a serious occasion.* That's your sacrifice for your sins running away.

Other Levites come running to help bring the animal under control and lead it to the altar. They work together to get it secured and the process proceeds. Your priest walks to the altar to officiate the sacrifice. He is too short to reach the bullock. He turns and walks into the temple. You wait, wondering what is going to take place next. He returns carrying a small stool and places it before the altar. He steps up onto the stool and proceeds to sacrifice the animal.

It is now time for the priest to do the heave offering. He cuts the shoulder of the animal and tries to lift it over his head. He falls backward off his stool, with the large shoulder portion landing on top of him. All you can see is the huge portion of meat and legs kicking. Levites come running to lift the offering from the priest's body. I realize all of this sounds ridiculous, but it shows why a dwarf was not allowed to serve in the office of a priest in the Old Testament.

What does God want us to understand today by refusing to allow Aaron's seed to minister if he were a dwarf? Today we need to see the spiritual type in the lives of those who are leading.

A dwarf is a human being, animal, or plant that is stunted in its growth. We are specifically talking about the priesthood. To be dwarfed is not growing into the stature of the parents, but missing that measure entirely. The priests born to Aaron and his sons were not to be dwarfs, but were to grow into the stature of the parent. Likewise, it is the intention that all the sons of our Great High priest, Jesus, should come into His stature.

> *Till we all come in the unity of the faith and of the knowledge of the Son of God, to a perfect man, to the measure of the stature of the fullness of Christ* (Ephesians 4:13).

The reason we can grow is because the seed remains in us. Jesus Christ is that Seed. First John 3:9 says, *"Whoever has been born of God does not sin, for His seed remains in him; and he cannot sin, because he has been born of God."* The word translated *seed* here is the Greek word *sperma,* from which we get the English word *sperm*. God's *sperma* or DNA creates the new creature, the believer. Then we are to grow into the stature of the fullness of Christ spiritually.

My wife and I have four children, two girls and two boys. I loved to see my children laugh and play as babies, as 5-year-olds, and at age 10 and then 20. Yet when they were 20 and of adult stature, I no longer treated them as 5-year-olds. They chose to get married and have families of their own. I would have been really concerned if they would have stopped growing at 5 years and never developed a vocabulary above that age level.

Alex Ness states:

> The Church is full of dwarfs. Generally the pastors must share some of that responsibility because they have not seen the membership as children, young men and fathers (1 John 2:12-14). The young men and fathers are given the same food as the children. They are not exercised or challenged to mature and do the works worthy of young men or fathers, resulting in spiritual pygmies sitting in the pews and eventually vacating them.
>
> How sad it is to see fifty-year old babies who must be entertained, cajoled, flattered, wheeled, coaxed, charmed, pampered, nursed and pled with to get them to a Sunday night service or mid week prayer meeting. They are two short in commitment, and love to be able to stand tall in service. Can you imagine a dwarf trying to kill a bullock or placing it on the Brazen Altar, or even attending to the Table of Showbread, Candlestick or Altar of Incense?[1]

When the Israelites came up to the Jordan River the first time, Moses sent 12 spies across into the land to look it over and bring back a report. They evidently spread out over the land in pairs and came back with their reports. They reported that the land was fantastic. The grapes were so big it took two men to carry a bough. They reported that the land flowed with milk and honey—a statement to them that meant it was a place of prosperity. You would think that this would be enough to get everyone excited and ready to run across the river and get their share.

What stopped them? The spies had very small spiritual insight. They came back with a report that they had seen giants in the land. They made a statement that showed their opinion of themselves and of their faith in God, "We were as grasshoppers in our sight and so we were in their sight." Notice that it was first their opinion of themselves that led them to be that way in the sight of others.

Many things can make you a spiritual dwarf. When you are dealing with an inferiority complex, it can lead to depression and discouragement. David said in Psalm 77:4, *"Thou holdest mine eyes waking: I am so troubled that I cannot speak"* (KJV). David is saying, "I had so many problems I couldn't talk!" No relief, can't sleep, too troubled to talk: sounds like a turtle crossing the road and seeing a 2,000 pound car coming at him. All he can do is hide in his shell, and hope. There are times when words seem inadequate. Those are times when we are overcome by depression and discouragement.

If you want to grow, you must develop a relationship with God based on His Word. Growth is not becoming more saved, more converted, or more justified, because when God saved you He did a complete job. You cannot be one-quarter saved or one-half saved. You are either justified and righteous or you are not.

When a baby is born we expect growth. If a baby doesn't grow you know something is wrong. So for the new believer we expect growth, and then maturity.

> *You therefore, beloved, since you know this beforehand, beware lest you also fall from your own steadfastness, being led away with the error of the wicked; but grow in the grace and knowledge of our Lord and Savior Jesus Christ. To Him be the glory both now and forever. Amen* (2 Peter 3:17-18).

In these verses we are asked to grow. Our desire should be to grow up into the Lord, not just be satisfied with being saved and never launching out!

There are some things we must forsake to grow. Certain relics of childhood must be put away. *"When I was a child, I spoke as a child, I understood as a child, I thought as a child; but when I became a man, I put away childish things"* (1 Cor. 13:11). The word *childish* is a Greek word for infant. Children play with toy cars, adults the real thing. Children play with dolls, and adults have real babies From infant to adult. Growing means outgrowing old clothes and getting new ones. We are expected to grow spiritually and put off immaturity.

Anything that will stop you from growing needs to be put away. I can no longer wear the slacks I wore when I was a teenager, I have outgrown them with age and maturity. Proper food is necessary to grow. You need to be feeding your spirit and mind. The Word of God is not skim milk, or one percent; it is whole milk and vitamin D enriched—enriched with Doctrine, Deliverance, Delight, and the Divine.

We cannot become too busy for a devotional life. Have you ever had a day when you were too busy to eat? When we rush through life and are empty inside, we snack on things without nutrition. David said, *"Your word have I hidden in my heart that I might not sin against You"* (Ps. 119:11).

Remove anything from your life that will stunt your growth in God. You don't want to be one who doesn't measure up. I went to several theme parks with my children when they were younger. On many of the rides that they wanted to ride, there was a board with a measuring rod. It always said that "if you are not this tall then you will not be allowed on this ride." Each time one of the children was just short of the mark, they would become upset and disappointed. God has a measuring line also for your spiritual life as a leader, and if you are a dwarf spiritually then you can't ride.

When my daughter Felicia took her children to Sea World, her daughter Karissa could not ride a roller coaster because she was a half inch too short. So when they returned the next day, Karissa wore shoes with a thicker heel. She was now just tall enough to ride. After they got on the roller coaster, her mother realized why they had the height requirement. She then locked arms with her daughter to keep her safe.

What is the moral of this story? That if you are spiritually small because you haven't fed your spirit man, and you are more motivated by your emotions and attitudes than the spirit, you need to realize that life in the ministry is a roller coaster. If you are not careful, you will fall out on one of the steep drops or when it does a flip—just like some in the past have fallen out of the ministry because the ride was more than they expected.

If you allow yourself to become small in your spirit man, then you are in danger of having what the apostle Paul called *"a form of godliness but denying its power"* (2 Tim. 3:5). The word *form* is an "image or outward appearance," having only the outward appearance of following the Gospel. The Pharisees were holy, but Jesus was godly. They knew the truth of godliness, but denied it.

We live in a society where young men are shot for their boom box or tennis shoes. But this is not the world that Paul was talking about; he was referring to the church world. He says that we can come to the place where we only have a form of godliness. Godliness is piety, devotion, reverence for God, a God-likeness or deep reverence for God!

Paul described the mystery of godliness as a personal relationship with Christ, the power of Christ and His resurrection (see 1 Tim. 3:16). It is not measured by temporal means. Ungodliness is just the opposite. It is defined as those who are controlled by their own natural desires and don't have the spirit.

If you find yourself in this state, it is not hopeless! The Bible tells us that you can develop godliness. *"As His divine power has given to us all things that pertain to life and godliness, through the knowledge of Him who called us by glory and virtue"* (2 Pet. 1:3).

The Scriptures here in Second Peter 1 continue to tell us that He has given us precious promises so we can become partakers of that divine nature. If you are diligent you can add to your faith virtue and then to your virtue knowledge. That means you should exercise your faith to develop virtue or excellence. Then from this excellence develop or gain knowledge that in turn will help you exercise self-control. Then with self-control comes the ability to be steadfast. Then having patience you will develop godliness—a reverence of God!

So godliness is a combination of salvation, promises, full personal relationship, diligence, faith, virtue, knowledge, self-control, steadfastness, and the life-changing force of Christ.

ENDNOTE

1. Ness, 139.

REVIEW QUESTIONS

1. What do you think is meant by "God's seed in us"?

2. What kind of insight did the spies have that came back to report on the Promised Land?

3. What are some of the things we must forsake in order to grow?

4. Godliness is a combination of what characteristics?

CHAPTER 11

A BLEMISH IN THE EYE

"For any man who has a defect shall not approach: . . . a man who has a defect in his eye. . . ." —Leviticus 21:18,20

This simply means that the priest must not have defective eyes. If the eyes were crossed or had cataracts, or any blemish, such conditions would disqualify the candidate. Crossed eyes or a lazy eye is associated with reduction of depth perception and, if onset is in adulthood, double vision.

In my early years of ministry there was a pastor whom I greatly respected. He had built a church of nearly 1,000 people. Today that doesn't sound like a great figure among all the megachurches, but this was an accomplishment for the late 1960s and early '70s.

In my opinion this pastor had one problem that eventually destroyed the great work that God intended to do with his life. His real desire was to be a businessman. He eventually started several businesses. He had an auction, a wholesale store, a restaurant, and several apartment houses. Before long these businesses demanded more and more of his time.

There were times when I would attend service and the deacons would come up to me and say, "The pastor isn't here. Will you preach tonight?" This happened on numerous occasions, on both Wednesday services and Sunday services. Over a few years the church fell from hundreds in attendance to 69 faithful followers.

The problem was double vision! The pastor was a spiritually cross-eyed priest. He had his eyes on the world and its success while trying to see God's vision for his life. He lost his focus! Jesus himself stressed the importance of the eye in Matthew 6:22-24:

> *The light of the body is the eye: if therefore thine eye be single, thy whole body shall be full of light. But if thine eye be evil, thy whole body shall be full of darkness. If therefore the light that is in thee be darkness, how great is that darkness! No man can serve two masters: for either he will hate the one, and love the other; or else he will hold to the one, and despise the other. Ye cannot serve God and mammon* (KJV).

Dr. Ness in his book *Holiness* says of this text:

> The reference to the eye is a reference to a lamp LUCHNOS that is fed by oil, and if not maintained can go out. The renewing of the Holy Spirit is a constant must or very soon we do not see things as clearly as we should. We have all seen this phenomenon pertaining to holiness. When a person first gets saved, their eyes are open and searching the Scriptures for light and truth. They are eager to abstain from the very appearance of evil. But as time goes by and they have winked at many things, you see their vision growing dim and they start overlooking things that were once important. Their eyesight should have become more keen to God's requirements and standards of holiness, but rather it grows dim.[1]

"But Jesus said to him, 'No one, having put his hand to the plow, and looking back, is fit for the kingdom of God'" (Luke 9:62). When you plow a field you have to look ahead at your goal and keep your eyes on that spot. If you look back or to the side you will plow uneven rows.

When you are cross-eyed you are trying to focus on two points at the same time. This confuses the brain. Eventually the brain will shut down one of the eyes in order to focus on a single object. *Webster's Dictionary* defines *cross-eye* as "an abnormal condition in which the eyes are turned toward each other; convergent strabismus; esotropia."

The downfall of King Saul was getting his eyes off of God and His purpose for his life and wanting the favor of the people. First Samuel 15:24 says, *"Then Saul said to Samuel, 'I have sinned, for I have transgressed the commandment of the Lord and your words, because I feared the people and obeyed their voice.'"* You cannot serve God and man both, this is double vision.

The Word says it this way.

> *Not with eyeservice, as men-pleasers, but as bondservants of Christ, doing the will of God from the heart* (Ephesians 6:6).

> *Bondservants, obey in all things your masters according to the flesh, not with eyeservice, as men-pleasers, but in sincerity of heart, fearing God* (Colossians 3:22).

We compromise in order to be accepted or liked and compromise in order not to offend. We fear proclaiming the Word and Jesus because we might offend someone.

The kind of service that seeks to catch the eye of people is rendering service for recognition. Whether one is seen or recognized should be immaterial. The important thing in service is holiness in our attitude. We do it because it is right for servants to serve God.

Jesus said in Luke 2:49, *"...I must be about My Father's business."* You need a *must* in your heart! I have preached conferences on the subject of lust in the heart, but neglected the subject of **must** in the heart. The Greek word for *must* is *dei* and it means "necessary." To me, the word implies urgency; more than just a desire, a drive, and a compulsion; a have to, an obligation, a requirement of life. I must eat to live; I must drink to live. Like a drug addict must have a fix, I must be about my Father's business!

It is interesting to see that the first recorded words of Jesus Christ are about His desire to fulfill His destiny. He must be about the Father's business. Others may play, others may do other things, but I must be about His business. Now that is singleness of vision. Jesus said in John 9:4, *"I must work the works of Him who sent Me while it is day; the night is coming when no one can work."* And in Luke 4:43: *"I must preach the kingdom of God to the other cities also, because for this purpose I have been sent."*

Leader, your life should be, *I must, I must, I must* have a compulsion to do the Father's business. The pressures of this world change us, sometimes from the power of Pentecost in our life to an intellectual faith. You may not have been called by an angelic visitation. It might not have been by vision like Ezekiel or by some great voice from Heaven. What you should have had is a must in your heart to do God's business: a divine compulsion. Keep your eyes on the goal and pay attention.

Once when the district secretary and I were traveling to Canada for a men's conference, we were into a heavy discussion when I realized that I was 15 miles past my exit. I looked at him and said, "Don't worry, there's another route we can take up the road about ten miles; don't let me miss it." Well, about three miles before the new route, he asked me a question and we started into another topic. Before I realized, it we were lost again. Keep your eyes on the goal and don't get distracted or let your eyes wander off the goal.

Another sign of being blemished in vision is listening to a second word and getting distracted from your purpose. When King Solomon died and his kingdom was divided, two tribes went with his son and ten tribes went with Jeroboam.

Jeroboam was afraid that the ten tribes that were then known as the kingdom of Israel would be persuaded to return to the other two tribes because they would go up to Jerusalem to worship God at His temple. So he created two golden calves and told the Israelites that the calves were their gods and they were to worship at these altars from then on. One calf was placed in Dan and the other in Bethel. We could be amazed by this, but people make up their own religious beliefs today based on what they want and not what the Word of God says. This is what Jeroboam found easy to do!

Then in First Kings 13, God sent His servant, a *"man of God,"* to reprimand Jeroboam while he was worshiping his golden calf. This man was being obedient to God in the face of grave opposition. The king was worshiping at the time and the man of God just walked up before the crowd and spoke to the altar. The king put out his hand to stop the prophet and his hand withered. This got the king's attention, and he pleaded for a healing of his hand. God healed the king's hand, but then the king tried to bribe the man of God. The man of God said, "No, I will not eat with you." He was saying, "No, the world cannot bribe me. I don't care whom I offend or what you offer, I won't give in!"

Had he stayed, he might have compromised his message! His actions would have made people think that maybe it wasn't as serious as it seemed; after all, he was eating with the king. This man would not be distracted from his goal. His vision was sure and single.

The unbeliever could not cause this man of God to sin, but another believer, a former prophet like himself, did. Not much was said about this man. Perhaps he had been in one of the schools of prophets under Samuel not many years before.

Just think. All the king's riches, fame, and glory could not defeat him in his obedience to the word of God given to him. It was a strange word that God had spoken to him. God had said, "Do not eat in the land and do not go home by the same road." But a second word from a man obviously not having the mind of the Spirit of God was able to accomplish what the king could not.

Some people amaze me: They hear from God, but because other believers don't understand what the Spirit is doing in their lives, they are persuaded to surrender. Another believer came who told this man of God he had an angel standing beside him to tell him that this man was to come home with him and eat. So the man of God believed the second word, and it cost him his life. Having good eyesight requires discernment! When God gives directions, don't go looking for confirmation from another person. Playing God in other people's lives is serious business!

Speaking of blemished eyes, Dr. Ness states:

> The Christ of Rev. 5:6 is seen as having seven eyes, which are the seven Spirits of God sent forth into all the earth. There is no winking of the eyes, shortsightedness or infirmity in the eyes of the Lord. How could a priest with blemishes in his eyes be representative of the Lord?

What you need is found in Revelation 3:18:

> *I counsel you to buy from Me gold refined in the fire, that you may be rich; and white garments, that you may be clothed, that the shame of your nakedness may not be revealed;* ***and anoint your eyes with eye salve****, that you may see.*

Ask the Father to heal your spiritual vision, to give you singleness of vision and heart. *"No man that warreth entangleth himself with the affairs of this life; that he may please Him who hath chosen him to be a soldier"* (2 Tim. 2:4 KJV).

Endnote

1. Ness, 140.

REVIEW QUESTIONS

1. What does it mean to be spiritually cross-eyed?

2. What was the downfall of King Saul?

3. What does it mean to have a *must* in your heart?

4. Has the enemy ever sent a second word into your heart to distract you?

Chapter 12

THE THIN-SKINNED

"For any man who has a defect shall not approach: ...a man who has...eczema or scab...."—Leviticus 21:18,20

At times I have sat in my office talking on the phone with a minister and I have listened to the hurt and anger pour out. I don't remember exactly what all the causes were now—it could have been about an insult someone said to him, or how another's words had torn him down. Someone didn't like the way he preached that weekend; he didn't dress to meet their standard; he should really try to coordinate better. A person didn't like the way his wife or one of his children acted. Maybe he preached too much from the Old Testament, or he had the wrong expression on his face. He may have appeared to someone to be condescending while he spoke, or he isn't paid to preach so hard against someone's personal sin. He took the offering wrong, he is unapproachable, or he is too familiar. This list of affronts could go on and on, but I think the point is made. This is church life and not everyone is going to be happy with you.

> *Yet hath he not root in himself, but dureth for a while: for when tribulation or persecution ariseth because of the word, by and by he is offende*d (Matthew 13:21 KJV).
>
> *Great peace have they which love Thy law: and nothing shall offend them* (Psalm 119:165 KJV).
>
> The New King James says, "*...nothing causes them to stumble.*"

The Words *Scurvy* and *Scabbed*

These words can denote almost any kind of skin disease. A *scab* could be a crust of a skin disease that is really caused by impurities in the blood.

Webster's Dictionary says that *scurvy* is "a disease characterized by swelling, hemorrhages, et cetera, caused by improper diet." Scurvy is a condition caused by a lack of vitamin C (ascorbic acid) in the diet. Signs of scurvy include tiredness, muscle weakness, joint pain and muscle aches, a rash on the legs, and bleeding gums. In the past, scurvy was common among sailors and other people deprived of fresh fruits and vegetables for long periods of time.

Scurvy is a disease of the blood that causes the blood to rise to the surface on the skin when it is touched. *Anemia* develops in 75% of patients as a result of blood loss into tissue, altered absorptions and metabolism of iron and foliate, gastrointestinal bleeding, and intravascular hemolysis (destruction of the red blood cells in the blood stream).

Scurvy shows us a leader who takes everything personally—who has anger or other emotions rise to the surface whenever confronted or rejected. If they don't get recognized at a meeting, or if they don't get their hand shaken, they won't come back.

If you are always taking offense or getting your feelings hurt, you have a problem with scurvy. Today we would say such people are thin-skinned.

Alex Ness says it this way:

> If scabs and scurvy appear on the outside, it is because the inside or the blood is unclean. That crusty, cranky person who is so hard to get along with has problems on the inside. Those bleeding hearts that you cannot touch or correct have deep spiritual problems. Preachers handle them with kid gloves lest they become wounded and bleed. They are in the choir, especially when they cannot carry a tune in a bucket. The musicians who play out of tune and

> beat because we are scared that some old wound may be opened. Someone was missed in special recognitions, they were overlooked at a party, their name was not submitted for the Board, the women's auxiliary or youth council. And what happens? The scurvy shows up. Their problem is much more deep rooted than what appears on the surface. We all need to be sanctified, cleansed and made holy by His precious blood.[1]

We, therefore, see why a priest who had impure blood and bled because of deficiency in vitamins would not qualify as a true representative of Christ or His priests.

There were no impurities in the precious blood of Jesus Christ. Because of His virgin birth He did not inherit the sin-stained blood of Adam. We who are sons of the Great High Priest are made nigh by the blood of Christ. Ephesians 2:13 says that the old covenant worshipers could only come near to God through the blood of atonement. The blood of Jesus purges us from all inward uncleanness making us holy before God.

> *And a servant of the Lord must not quarrel but be gentle to all, able to teach, patient, in humility correcting those who are in opposition, if God perhaps will grant them repentance, so that they may know the truth, and that they may come to their senses and escape the snare of the devil, having been taken captive by him to do his will* (2 Timothy 2:24-26).

Luke 17:1 explains more about what the snare of the devil is: *"It is impossible that no offenses should come, but woe to him through whom they do come!"* The word *offenses* comes from the Greek word *skandalon,* meaning "the part of the trap the bait was attached to." Offended people produce fruit such as hurt, anger, outrage, jealousy, resentment, strife, bitterness, hatred, and envy. The results of these are: insults, attacks, wounding, divisions, separation, broken relationships, betrayal, and backsliding.

When I think about all the ministers who have left the ministry each year, I ask myself how many had a problem with scurvy. Those who love the law of the Lord are not easily offended (see Ps. 119:165 KJV). This Scripture implies that the lack of time in the Word leads to spiritual immaturity. Proper spiritual nutrition is just as important as natural nutrition.

The answer to offenses is forgiveness! To be a spiritual leader who is used of God, you must be a person who is ready to forgive.

The altar where sacrifices unto God were made was created out of shittim wood. This wood was termite resistant. That means it is demon, gossip, and anger resistant. God had the Israelites make it out of wood that would not shrink, wood that would not swell up! We can't let the actions of others cause us to swell or grow angry. We can't let those actions cause us to shrink away and become timid and fearful. Only dead flesh can worship in fire.

Being offended can cause you to be easily deceived. It can cause the love of God to grow cold towards others. Cain is a good example of someone offended. He had made an offering to God and been rejected, while his brother Abel had sacrificed and been accepted. He let his jealousy burn within him. He meditated on his anger and began to resent his brother—and finally killed him.

You may say, "If it wasn't for those critical people in the church, I could praise the Lord! If it wasn't for deacon Jones, I could accomplish something in this church; he is holding my ministry back." Yet when you are too sensitive, you disqualify yourself from ministry. Leadership in the church is not all glorious. Most of the persecution you will suffer will come from those within, not those outside the church. The church membership is made up of a great many personalities, and not all of them are good.

Remember the pastor who sent me the résumé showing he had pastored nine churches in nine years? He evidently had a temperament that could not take conflict or personal affronts. When you let your emotions hang out on the surface of your personality, you are not fit to lead.

> *Behold, I have made thy face strong against their faces, and thy forehead strong against their foreheads. As an adamant* [diamond] *harder than flint have I made thy forehead: fear them not, neither be dismayed at their looks, though they be a rebellious house* (Ezekiel 3:8-9 KJV).

Ezekiel means "strengthened by God." So God spoke to him that he would make his strength of spirit and soul stronger than those he was called to. A stronger forehead is a metaphor concerning animals that butt their heads together like rams. One sure thing about leadership is that you will butt heads with others! It may be with a board over a new program you want. It may be over your vision for those you lead. It may be with an influential member in your group who is upset with you.

I have always dreaded those terrifying words, spoken at times just before I go to the pulpit for service: "You know I love you pastor, but I want to speak with you after service!" Then throughout the worship service and my sermon, I am trying to take my mind off the person's controversy.

Once a board member said to me, "I need to speak with you." He and his wife came to my office and proceeded to lay out 14 things that they didn't like about me. Not only did they have a list of 14 things such as, "We are offended by your facial expression when you preach, and we don't like the term *sinner;* you should use *unbeliever* as it is less offensive," but he informed me that he had gone to about 18 other church members to bounce it off them first, before coming to me.

Then the Spirit of God took over, and I thanked them for their concerns about me and informed them that I would pray about their concerns. Assuring them that if God informed me that they were right in any of these areas I would endeavor to change. This seemed to be the right answer and they were satisfied. I kept their list and prayed about all of the points they made. Did I feel they were right? No. But being obedient to the

Lord is more important than my ego. Once I prayed about it, I cast it aside and continued on with the vision.

I have always felt that if you are to offer rebukes as a leader, then you should also be willing to receive them with grace. This is not always pleasant. But those who love the Word of God are not easily offended!

God is able to change you and fortify your emotions and character. This is why He gave *gifts* unto men (see Eph. 4:7-16). This term in Ephesians implies character gifts. In other words, He gives the proper character to the person He calls. If He calls you to be an apostle, then He prepares you to be an apostle. If He calls you to be a pastor, then He will give you the pastor's nature, so you can stand against those who oppose you or speak ill of you, just as he did for Ezekiel. If you are easily offended, ask yourself whether you are called to make everybody happy or to do the will of the Father.

Some people may think what happens to you in life is payback. But really it's a set up for a strong comeback. It all comes down to your perception of the situation. Sometimes even tragedy is for a stronger calling. Many times the mountain that you are trying by faith to cast into the sea is meant for you to climb. It may be your next high place in God!

Pray and ask God to help you have the nature He has prepared for your ministry. Practice forgiveness and mercy to those you serve who offend you. Then take time in His Word and be in prayer. Did Moses have the right to be offended by his sister Miriam when she was telling him that he had the wrong wife and that God could use her and Aaron just as well as him?

God came down and told Miriam and Aaron that He had called Moses, that Moses was His friend, and that He would talk to him face to face. Then God struck Miriam with leprosy for speaking against His servant. What did Moses do? Did he say to himself, "Good. She got what she deserved!"? No, he interceded for the one who had insulted and demeaned him. Now that is forgiveness.

Moses was an example of God's meekness and mercy working thorough the life of a leader. One of the marks of the Spirit's fruit in your life is meekness and love. Immaturity is the lack of God's fruit in our lives. You cannot have scurvy and lead! If you are too touchy and easily offended, it's time you seek the Word of God for your life, not someone else's life. Turn the Word of God on your own life, instead of seeking the Word to justify yourself against those who have offended you.

We all face times of rebuke, hurt, offenses coming our way. The mark of a leader is not that he or she is never offended, but how he handles the offense.

You will be offended at one time or another. The measure of your leadership is how you handle that offense.

Endnote

1. Ness

REVIEW QUESTIONS

1. Do you know anyone in ministry who is too thin-skinned?

2. What kind of fruit do offended people produce?

3. As a leader are you called to make everyone happy?

4. What did Miriam do that could have offended Moses?

Chapter 13

THOSE WITH BROKEN STONES

"For any man who has a defect shall not approach: a man who....is a eunuch...."—Leviticus 21:18,20

Several years ago, I was serving our district as the secretary treasurer. The bishop decided that we should fly to the general board meetings in Joplin, Missouri. This required a flight from our small local airport to Washington DC, then a flight to St. Louis, and another flight into Joplin. The trip out was uneventful, but the return flights were all behind schedule. We flew out of Joplin late, and when we rushed to the next flight, there were only three seats left. We were separated into different sections of the plane. Then we were informed that the airline had to find pilots because of a scheduling error. The plane sat for over an hour waiting for pilots.

During this time I was seated between two young people. One was a young woman who was the daughter of missionaries to Africa. The other was a young man flying home from college on break. I settled back and closed my eyes for a nap, when the Holy Spirit spoke to me and said, "Ask the young man if he wants to get saved." I turned to him and asked the question. He threw his hands into the air and said, "I give up! My mother is after me at home to get saved. I go off to college and my roommate is a Christian and is always asking me to get saved. I get on an airplane and the guy next to me asks me to get saved. I give up, help me get saved."

We both got down on our knees in the plane and asked Christ into his heart. God gloriously saved the young man. When we got off the plane he brought his mother and father over to see me at the baggage claim. Then He called me two weeks later and told me he had joined his mother's church.

Alex Ness states the following concerning Leviticus 21:20:

> Reference is made here to the genital parts or reproductive organs. If by crushing, bruising, cutting or in any way the reproductive organs are deemed ineffective, that son of Aaron could not qualify for the priesthood. God made man and woman to multiply and replenish the earth. An

inability to do so would not properly represent the Lord whose seed shall be as the sand of the sea. *"As the host of heaven cannot be numbered, neither the sand of the sea measured; so will I multiply the seed of David my servant, and the Levites that minister unto me."* (Jer. 33:22 KJV)

An ability to reproduce and have many children was considered a great blessing. One of the promises made to and reward to Abraham for his faith and obedience was that his seed would multiply.

"That in blessing I will bless thee, and in multiplying I will multiply thy seed as the stars of the heaven, and as the sand which is upon the sea shore; and thy seed shall possess the gate of his enemies; and in thy seed shall all the nations of the earth be blessed; because thou has obeyed my voice." (Gen. 22:17-18 KJV) The same promise was made to Isaac in Gen. 26:24 and to Israel in Lev. 26:9.

The believers in Christ are Abraham's seed. *"And if ye be Christ's, then are ye Abraham's seed, and heirs according to the promise."* (Gal. 3:29)

Brother Ness continues by stating:

There are many references to being productive:

"I am the vine, ye are the branches." (John 15:5).

What are the branches to do? Bear much fruit. If not, they are cut off and burned.

> *"Herein is my Father glorified, that ye bear much fruit; so shall ye be my disciples."* (John 15:8) and *"Ye have not chosen me, but I have chosen you, and ordained you, that ye should go and bring forth fruit, and that your fruit should remain; that whatsoever ye shall ask of the Father in my name, He may give it you."* (John 15:16)[1]

A spiritual leader will be a person who can reproduce himself or herself. I believe this statement applies to two areas that a leader must consider. First, every believer is called to be a minister of reconciliation and needs to be fulfilling the great commission. Before you can lead others to share and win the lost to Jesus, you should already be a soul winner yourself.

I was talking to a young man recently who stated that he had been in rehab, trying to get free from drugs. He said that a new drug counselor had just started work at the rehab. He had never used drugs and had never tasted alcohol. Now that's not a bad thing! However if you are going to be a drug counselor to those who are addicted, you need to understand where they are coming from. The young man said that no one respected the counselor or listened to him. The counselor left within two weeks. To lead other believers and have never fulfilled the great commission yourself would be a shame.

In many churches today salvation isn't even approached from the podium. There is never an altar call for people to repent and find Jesus. This is not Christian leadership. How can a man or woman pastor a congregation who has never lead a person to Jesus?

Years ago when I was starting out in ministry, I would take Mondays off for a family day. We couldn't afford to do more than window shop or take the children to the park. We were at the park one day watching our children play on the playground equipment, when a young man walked up to me and handed me a tract. I thought I would have a little fun with him, so I asked him what the paper was for.

He responded that it was about changing my life and accepting Christ as my savior. I asked, "Why do I need to do that?" He replied that the Bible said that all men were under sin, because of Adam's sin in the garden. I asked, "Where does it say that?" He began to search for the Scripture. I asked, "Is that in Romans?" He said, "Yes, you are right," and proceeded to look in the book of Romans. Suddenly he looked up and asked, "Are you a Christian already?" I replied, "Yes, I am." We both laughed and I shared with him that I was proud of him for sharing the Gospel of Jesus with others.

When I found Jesus as my Savior, the first thing that I wanted to do was share that joy. I would go witnessing and handing out tracts in the malls every weekend. I witnessed to those I worked with, knocked on doors, and invited people to our church. My greatest joy was leading someone in the sinner's prayer. My area supervisor would come to our store where I worked and ask, "Has Rick got you saved yet?"

One of the problems of witnessing is believability. When Mary came to the tomb of Jesus and found it empty, she ran and told the disciples. They didn't believe her (see Mark 16:11)—perhaps because women were not allowed to be witnesses at that time of history, or because the story was too unbelievable for them. They told the other disciples and they didn't believe. Finally Jesus showed Himself to everyone except Thomas. When the others shared with Thomas, he still didn't believe. Jesus said, *"You have seen and believe, blessed are they which have not seen and believe"* (see John 20:29). You have to believe, before anyone will believe you.

To witness comes from a Greek word *martyron*. It is the word we get *martyr* from—which makes me think that witnessing requires dying to ourselves, to love souls of others, to die to our fears and dislikes.

We must first realize all of the unchurched are not alike. Jesus did this when He said to the Canaanite woman, *"I am sent to the lost sheep of Israel"* (see Matt. 15:24). Matthew's Gospel was written to the Hebrews, Mark's Gospel was to the Gentile reader, Peter was sent to the Jew, and Paul was sent to the Gentiles. If you are an intellectual you will relate better to intellectuals. If you are a farmer you will relate best to farmers, if you are a mechanic you may relate best to mechanics, etc. The Gospel is spread primarily through relationships.

When Andrew heard of Christ, he went and told his brother Simon Peter. When Philip found Christ, he went to his friend Nathaniel. When Matthew the tax collector found Christ, he held an evangelistic dinner party for other tax collectors. The woman at the well told everyone in her village about Christ.

Sometimes, in order to reach the place where people are in need, we have to lighten the ship. In Acts 27:18-26 the apostle Paul is in the midst of a terrible storm. The ship is in danger of being lost at sea. But God has let the apostle know that it is His will that the ship be cast upon a certain island.

The needs on this island were many, and God needed to show His power to the lost. A man there was dying of bloody flux and fever. There were many sick on the island in need of God's healing. Plus everyone on the island needed the Gospel message and to find Jesus. The world today is in need!

Many today cannot reach them because they have too much in the boat. The closer to the island, the shallower the water. The lighter the boat, the less likely you are to be grounded before you reach the place of need. Many cannot go to the needs of others because they are so loaded down themselves. They cannot reach others; they beach their boat. The storms of life help to unload a lot of stuff.

My family and I were visiting Rehoboth beach one summer. My son Jason and I were riding the surf into the beach using boogie boards. We did this for hours until our bodies were raw from landing in the surf.

The next year we returned to the beach and we rented two boogie boards and went out to ride the waves. The waves would pick Jason up and ride him into the shore. But I just couldn't seem to catch a wave. No matter how hard I tried, it wouldn't work. It wasn't until we were finished and returning home that I figured out why I couldn't ride the board into the shore. The year before I weighed 179 pounds, but this year I weighed 210 pounds. I was too heavy for the waves. If I wanted to make it all the way to shore, I needed to lose 30 pounds.

Sometimes we do not reach the lost on the island because we are weighted down by so much stuff in our own lives. We carry emotional baggage. When King Saul was chosen as king he was hiding among the stuff, hiding from his responsibilities and call. James and John couldn't see the needs. They wanted to call down fire. Their pride and ego were weighing them down: the desire for attention, the desire for prominence, the desire for acclaim, the desire to be better than others, the desire to always be justified. Humility means to empty out the vessel.

SOMETIMES IT IS PHYSICAL BAGGAGE

The rich young ruler was carrying too much baggage. He couldn't let go of his possessions to follow Jesus. When the storms come, holding onto these things will make you sink. These sailors and Paul had to make a decision. Do I really need this suitcase if I sink? It's human nature to cling to objects, perhaps because of sentiment, or value, or security, or position.

Realize God will intervene to get you to the island to minister to the lost. Would God change the circumstance of many because of one? Yes. God did it to the ship that Jonah had boarded. They would have sunk because of his sin. God stopped all of Israel because of Achan and his secret sin. God wrecked Paul's ship just to reach the tribe that lived on that island.

God is concerned about souls. If you are not a soul-winner then it may be time to start lightening the ship.

The second area for a leader to master in order to reproduce himself or herself is making disciples for the ministry. Each creature produces after its kind, so a leader needs to reproduce himself. Those who are insecure in their ministries, who fear that every other person is out to take their ministry away from them, will not reproduce. They will not train others to succeed them. I have always said that no one can steal your ministry if you are called by God.

At one time I had nine preachers attending my church. I tried to have each one preach as often as I could. Once, at a minister's meeting, one of the brothers asked, "Aren't you afraid of sharing your pulpit so easily?" My response was that until God was finished with me as pastor, no one could take my God-given ministry; it was in His hands.

Discipleship was one of the last commands of our Lord before He ascended. It should be the desire of every to produce others to lead.

Endnote

1. Ness, 145.

REVIEW QUESTIONS

1. Does God expect us to reproduce ourselves spiritually?

2. What is one of the major problems with witnessing?

3. What is some of the baggage we carry with us that keeps us from helping others with their needs?

4. What is the second area of reproduction for a leader?

CHAPTER 14

THE QUALIFIED LEADER

With all of these disqualifications, then what kind of leader does qualify? Who would God entrust with the authority of His Kingdom? I believe these questions are answered in Matthew 16. Jesus asks His disciples who people say He is. They give the answer in verse 14: *"Some say that thou art John the Baptist: some, Elias; and others, Jeremias, or one of the prophets"* (KJV).

Then Jesus asks them, *"But whom say ye that I am?"* And Simon Peter answered and said, *"Thou art the Christ, the Son of the living God."* (Matt. 16:15-16 KJV).

The response of the Lord was *"Blessed art thou, Simon Barjona: for flesh and blood hath not revealed it unto thee, but My Father which is in heaven"* (Matt. 16:17 KJV). Right at this point in Peter's life he has proven that he is able to receive revelation from God. This impresses the Savior, and He states that He is giving Peter the keys to the Kingdom of Heaven so that whatever he binds on earth shall be bound in heaven and whatsoever he looses on earth shall be loosed in heaven.

Keys are a figurative term for authority or power. Peter is a representative of the preemptive New Testament Church. In biblical times a man showed his authority by wearing his keys on his shoulder. They carried their keys over their shoulder or pinned them there for others to see. The number of keys showed the amount of power and authority that you had over certain things. It implied authority, power, ownership, and riches. Isaiah gives us more insight to this practice: *"And the key of the house of David will I lay on his shoulder; so he shall open, and none shall shut; and he shall shut, and none shall open"* (Isa. 22:22 KJV).

At this point Peter is promised a pretty impressive anointing for ministry. But he begins to get a little lifted up from this blessing upon him in front of his peers. Just a few moments later he is trying to correct the Savior Himself. Jesus then has to rebuke him severely. *"But He turned, and said unto Peter, Get thee behind me, Satan: thou art an offence unto Me: for thou savourest not the things that be of God, but those that be of men"* (Matt. 16:23 KJV). From the head of the class to the detention hall in one breath. But that was Peter—impetuous and outspoken, acting before he thought things through.

As we look at the life of the man whom Jesus chose to carry the keys of the Kingdom, we see a man who will act on impulse and his emotions. When Jesus is accosted in the garden, it is Peter who draws a sword and cuts off the ear of the high priest's servant. *"Then Simon Peter having a sword drew it, and smote the high priest's servant, and cut off his right ear. The servant's name was Malchus"* (John 18:10 KJV). Later Peter follows Jesus to His trial with the high priest. While he is warming himself at the fire, he denies that he even knows Jesus. He eventually denies Jesus three times, and slips into his old nature and curses.

At this point Peter doesn't seem like the right choice for the man to carry God's authority. However, Jesus has not given up on Peter. After His resurrection He makes a point to seek Peter out. Peter has returned to his former occupation. Jesus finds him in a boat fishing. So now we see a man who has allowed his nature and attitudes to bring him down and in his disappointment he has returned to his former life.

In John 21, Jesus calls out from the shore and tells them to throw the net on the other side of the boat. At this point the net fills with fish and Peter realizes that it has to be Jesus. He jumps into the water and swims to the shore. Here Peter is confronted by Jesus. Jesus asks, *"Simon, son of Jonah, do you love Me more than these?"* (John 21:15).

Jesus is using the term *agapao* which means to "love affectionately, ardently, supremely, perfectly." Peter keeps using the Greek term *phileo* in response, which means "to love, to like, to regard, to feel friendship for another." Peter has boasted prior to his fall that all the others might desert Jesus but that he never would. Now he is asked, "Do you love Me more than these, like you said you did?" His response now is one of guilt and insecurity.

Jesus persists by asking him again, "Simon, son of Jonah, do you love Me?" This time He doesn't ask him if he loves more than others. Peter has been humbled, but now Jesus persists until the third time and Peter is grieved. He has denied Jesus three times and now has to relive his sin until he is grieved by his sin.

After the day of Pentecost, Peter, who has now been filled with the Spirit, steps forward to speak to the crowd and uses the keys to open the door of the Kingdom to 3,000 souls.

What brought about this change? First was repentance and a renewed commitment to Jesus. Second was the enduing of power from the Holy Spirit.

From this point we see a great commitment to faithfulness in Peter's life. This attitude is found throughout the great men and women of the Bible. Elisha was willing to burn his plow and sacrifice his oxen to follow Elijah. Ruth cleaved to Naomi, declaring that Naomi's God was her God. We look at men like Paul, who were shipwrecked, stoned, and beaten, but who never stopped and stayed committed to the paths that God had chosen for them.

This attitude is not saying, "God, this is where I will serve You." It is not telling God, "These are my conditions of service." What is the attitude of ministry? It is saying, "Not my will but Thine be done, Lord," or "Here am I, Lord, send me!" *"My heart is steadfast, O God, my heart is steadfast; I will sing and give praise"* (Ps. 57:7).

Elisha was committed to a goal, and he showed consistency. He would not stop each time Elijah said to him, "Elisha, stay here while I go on." He had a purpose in mind; He knew his calling. He remembered the day, years before, when the mantle was placed on his shoulders. I have seen so many start the path, only to fall along the way. On fire one day and cold the next. Hebrews 10:23 states, *"Let us hold fast the profession of our faith without wavering; (for He is faithful that promised)"* (KJV).

Webster defines *consistency* as "no contradiction, stay harmonious, conforming to a single set of principles." Not up and down, changing with a new revelation each week, but consistent, walking on solid ground, built upon the foundation of the apostles.

Committed, consistent, and full of spiritual discernment. Elijah said, "You can only have this power you ask for if you have the discernment to see me when I go." We are living in a day when even the very elect can be deceived. There are fakes everywhere—on the screen, in books, on the radio, and in churches—deceiving the children of God. One of the greatest needs of the ministry today is a person of discernment.

In Luke 9:23 Jesus said, "*...Let him deny himself, and take up his cross daily, and follow Me.*" A leader needs to come to a place of self-denial. The path that Jesus walked was a life of self-denial. If you want to do the works that Jesus did, you have to follow the pattern that Jesus laid down, such as a life of prayer. Not just five minutes a day. I read a survey in a Christian periodical once that surveyed Christian leaders concerning their prayer life. After everything was averaged out, the average prayer time was five minutes a day.

Self would rather turn over in bed and say, "I must get my rest." Jesus would get up a great while before day and depart into a solitary place where He would pray.

Once I received a call from a pastor asking me to come minister at his church. He stated that everything was in turmoil, the crowds were falling off, there was back biting, and that he was giving it one more chance. I started on Sunday night and could feel the bondage in the service.

After service I informed the pastor that I would like to stay in the church for the night. After everyone left I began to do spiritual warfare for the church. I prayed until about 11:30P.M. and lay down on one of the pews to rest. I dosed off, and at midnight the Holy Spirit woke me up. I heard Him say, "Wake up, it is time to do battle." I got up and suddenly I felt the presence of a strong evil spirit enter the church. A voice spoke and said, "What are you doing in my church, puny preacher?" I replied,

"I'm here to kick you out and retake what belongs to God's children." I began to bind and loose and rebuke this spirit. God revealed to me that it was a territorial spirit over that area of the city. After about three hours of prayer the battle was won. That next night revival broke out in the church and restoration happened.

The prayer of a saint who believes in the power of prayer is the greatest outlet of power on earth. Peter understood the power of prayer and fasting, having been taught repeatedly by his Lord. Peter recommitted his life to Jesus, and walked with commitment, consistency, and spiritual discernment. He was a man of like passions, just like you or me. Repentance and surrender qualified him to carry the keys of the Kingdom.

That is all that God requires of us. Evaluate your life and surrender, letting God put off the old and put on the new.

REVIEW QUESTIONS

1. What do keys represent in the Bible?

2. What should be the attitude of those in ministry?

3. What is one of the greatest outlets of power in a believer's life?

4. What do you feel is the difference between commitment and consistency?

CHAPTER 15

THE PERSON GOD BLESSES

In Genesis 6:1-22 we find that God was grieved in His spirit that He had made man. He decided to destroy humankind off the face of the earth. Then he found one man, Noah, who was righteous and decided to bless him. In verse 22 it says, *"Thus Noah did; according to all that God commanded him, so he did."* God spoke to Noah and gave him instructions, and then we see Noah's first attribute that caused him to be used of God.

FAITHFULNESS

God enabled Noah to serve Him in the midst of the wickedest generation on the earth. God is able to do that for us. God gives more grace when sin abounds—the more sin comes against you, the more grace God will use to keep you. You can faithfully serve God.

God's service is based upon faithfulness. When my children were small, I would ask them to clean their rooms. When Felicia was 14 and Nathan was 4, I expected more out of Felicia than I did Nathan. However, both of them received the same reward. The reward was based upon their faithfulness and their ability at the time.

Second, the person whom God blesses hears from God. Genesis 6:13 says, *"And God said to Noah...."* Faithfulness is the foundation. It is the door that enables us to hear what God is saying. This requires that we commune with Him regularly. There is always time to talk to Jesus.

Then we see that a person whom God blesses obeys God regardless. Imagine how God's instructions sounded to Noah. First Noah was bound by the present-day knowledge. He could not understand nor expect rain. And he had never even heard of a flood. It takes special men or women with direction from God to do the miraculous. Columbus was taught that the earth was flat, but he believed the Bible. Noah rejected the word of others regardless, because he had heard from God. I'm sure he was called foolish and crazy by the society he lived in.

The Bible is not a book of logic or reason, or even of common sense at times. After all, here we see God brought water to the boat, not the boat to water. We must obey regardless of the world's reasoning. We must believe that God can prosper us, that faith works, that God heals today, that there is power in Him to overcome all things. The kind of person that God blesses does what God wants regardless.

Have you ever thought about the ridicule Noah and his family received? I am Noah's wife was ridiculed at the "grocery store." People looked at her thinking, *That poor woman married to that nut Noah. All he wants to do is preach judgment and everybody knows that God is love. He's wasting all their money on that huge boat. I'd divorce him in a minute if he were my husband.*

Then there were people who spoke to the sons and daughters-in-law. "Hey what's your father-in-law doing out there? Do you think your husband will inherit his father's insanity?"

And yet Noah was faithful. He persisted in proclaiming the word God had given him. After nearly 100 years his ministry only produced eight people. Now that's faithfulness. God is still looking for the leaders who will hear from Him and proclaim the Word, by their lives and lips.

The result of such faithfulness was that Noah secured the reward that was promised by God. He had heard the Lord speak to him—and we do not read of God speaking again to him until it was time to load the ark. What was his obligation? It was to do what God had told him until God said otherwise. He did that and remained faithful to his calling.

How do you get in God's favor and blessing? You faithfully serve God. You listen to God. You obey God regardless of circumstances. You persistently proclaim the Gospel message and then you will secure your reward.

REVIEW QUESTIONS

1. What is God speaking to your heart that you need to be more faithful in?

2. As you look over your past, what happened when you were faithful?

3. In what ways to you think God enabled Noah to be faithful?

4. What was Noah's reward for faithfulness? Do you think there are more rewards of faithful living? If so, list several.

Chapter 16

HOW TO MAINTAIN THE ANOINTING

As a young evangelist I was asked to accompany a more seasoned evangelist to help with a crusade in the Bahamas. Needing money for this trip, I approached a pastor of a large church and asked if I could use his auditorium for a service to help raise funds. The Saturday night service was scheduled, and advertising was placed on the radio and in the newspapers. The night of the service the turnout was really great. We had a singing group minister, and then I preached. About 20 people responded to the altar call.

I went to the pastor and asked if he would like for me to do a follow-up meeting from Sunday through Wednesday to help draw in the new converts. He gave his consent. Well, the first night of the meeting, God's presence never seemed to arrive. Preaching was like reading out of a dictionary: very dry. It was the only time I can remember not giving an invitation or altar call of some kind.

The next day I went to the church early and lay prostrate before the Lord and asked Him what had gone wrong. The Spirit spoke to me and said, "I just wanted you to try it without Me one time." I repented of my pride and ambition that day and asked God to never leave me alone like that again. I have carried that fear with me ever since. It is a terrible thing to trust in yourself and not have the anointing.

As preachers we often talk about "the anointing." We pray for the anointing of God on our lives, our ministries, our activities, on everything. We recognize that we need the power and presence of the Holy Spirit or our efforts are worthless. Zechariah 4:6 says, *"... 'Not by might nor by power, but by my Spirit,' says the Lord of hosts."* We must minister in the power of God, under His anointing of the Holy Spirit. The question was asked to me recently, "How do you maintain the anointing in your life?"

First let's look at what the word *anointing* means. There are many Hebrew and Greek words in relation to the anointing: The word *mashach* means "to rub with oil, to consecrate and to paint."

The word *cwk,* pronounced "sook," means "to smear over." Then the Greek word *murizoz* means "to apply." The basic meaning of the word *anoint* is simply to smear something on an object. Usually oil is involved, but it could be other substances such as paint or dye. This gives the idea that to anoint something or someone is an act of consecration. In simple terms, the anointing is the presence of the Holy Spirit being smeared upon someone.

Jesus is our example in Luke 4:18-19:

> *The Spirit of the Lord is upon Me, because He has anointed Me to preach the gospel to the poor; He has sent Me to heal the brokenhearted; to proclaim liberty to the captives and recovery of sight to the blind, to set at liberty those who are oppressed; to proclaim the acceptable year of the Lord.*

> Isaiah 10:27: *It shall come to pass in that day that his burden will be taken away from your shoulder, and his yoke from your neck, and the yoke shall be destroyed because of the anointing oil.*

I believe that to answer the question of how to maintain the anointing, it will help to explain God's recipe for the anointing oil from Exodus 30:22-25:

> *Moreover the Lord spake unto Moses, saying, Take thou also unto thee principal spices, of pure myrrh five hundred shekels, and of sweet cinnamon half so much, even two hundred and fifty shekels, and of sweet calamus two hundred*

> *and fifty shekels, and of cassia five hundred shekels, after the shekel of the sanctuary, and of oil olive an hin: and thou shalt make it an oil of holy ointment, an ointment compound after the art of the apothecary: it shall be an holy anointing oil* (Exodus 30:22-25 KJV).

God was very specific about what He wanted in the anointing oil, and if any ingredient was missing from the oil, then that person was not anointed. This was the anointing oil for ministry and consecration. It was only to be used for this purpose and never on a stranger. The spices had to be of quality. The Hebrew word *roshe* meaning "the head, the chief, the first or excellent" was used. With God's anointing there is no generic brand. These ingredients were not common or cheap. They were valuable, costly, and rare.

In God's anointing oil, which was to be rubbed on or poured on, were four spices—myrrh, cinnamon, calamus, and cassia—plus olive oil. The number *five* in the Bible speaks of grace. Grace means God's favor. God knows that humankind had become weak after the fall. Therefore, He yearns to supply us with His Spirit, the anointing, to favor His children with His ability and strength to reenforce our lives.

The Spice Called Myrrh

Myrrh is a pale yellow gummy substance or liquid from a small thorny shrub, which grows in Somalia, Ethiopia, and Arabia. The word *myrrh* means "pure or free flowing." It is purifying in its application. The fire of the Holy Spirit is not for our destruction but for our purification. Purification comes from the death of the old man. To get the sweetness out of myrrh you had to crush it. It was always used to anoint people for burial. So it speaks of purity and death in our lives.

This implies that to have the anointing in your life, you must crucify the old man with Jesus and be living in the new man in pureness and holiness. Second Timothy 2:21 says, *"If a man therefore purge himself from these, he shall be a vessel unto honour, sanctified, and meet for the Master's use, and prepared unto every good work"* (KJV).

Holiness is necessary to maintain your anointing! Holiness is the habit of being in one mind with God. It is the habit of agreeing in God's judgment, hating what He hates, loving what He loves, and measuring everything in this world by the standard of His Word.

The Spice Called Cinnamon

Cinnamon oil is distilled from the bark of the cinnamon tree growing in Ceylon. It is tasty and is usually used to flavor food because of its pleasant aroma. The fragrance was beautiful in the tabernacle because it counteracted the stench of the animal sacrifices.

It represents the ability to keep sweet in any circumstances. God says not to revile when you are reviled, to bless those who curse you. This keeps bitterness, anger, unforgiveness, hurt, and anguish out of your life, because of your relationship with Jesus Christ.

Maintaining your anointing means to stay sweet and not become bitter. There are many opportunities in ministry to become wounded, rejected, or disappointed. Each of these can cause you to have your anointing blocked or weakened.

Solomon used cinnamon to perfume the bed of his lover. This is an illustration to us that cinnamon can represent our intimate relationship with our Savior. He is what keeps us sweet and sensitive. When you let your relationship with Christ wane, then you are moving out of the sweetness of your anointing and you are not maintaining the anointing in your life.

The Calamus or Cane Spice

Calamus is a sweet cane plant of about 10 feet high growing in marshy places in Asia. As it is crushed or broken it exudes a sweet fragrance. It speaks to us of brokenness. "*...But on this one will I look: on him who is poor and of a contrite spirit, and who trembles at My word*" (Isa. 66:2). The word *contrite* in Hebrew is *nakeh* meaning "smitten." A second word, *dakah,* means "to crumble, to bruise, to break into pieces."

The woman in Mark 14 brought an alabaster flask of spikenard (another name for the cane plant perfume). It is a very expensive and rare extract from a bearded grass growing in India.

How many years it took this woman to save the money to buy this is not known. But the cost was about 300 days of labor. The Bible says that she broke the flask, her life of sacrifice, and poured the contents on Jesus's head.

Can you imagine how sweet smelling a priest was when he was anointed with all this spicy mixture? People knew who the priest was by the smell of the anointing.

The force that can remove this aspect of your anointing is pride. Pride can prevent you from experiencing the benefits of brokenness. As long as a person keeps pride, he cannot carry a high level of anointing in his or her life. God's anointing on your life is His approval. God is regarding you with pleasure and respect and loves the sweet smell of His anointing on your life. Don't let pride sour the smell.

The Cassia Spice

Cassia is the aromatic bark of a tree growing in Arabia. It is also used by some doctors as medicine. It is derived from a Hebrew root word, *quadad,* meaning "to blend, to bow, or to stoop."

> *Therefore humble yourselves under the mighty hand of God, that He may exalt you in due time* (1 Peter 5:6).

Cassia speaks of humility in our lives. Submission to His will is the path to humility, and humility is the path to promotion. A continuous walk in humility will cause God's anointing to flow in an individual's life. All of the ingredients were mixed with olive oil.

The Olive Oil

The olive oil was one of the primary tree crops of ancient Israel. Consistently in the Bible the oil symbolizes the person of the Holy Spirit. He is the principle character in the anointing of God.

Look at the picture we have here. All of these ingredients mixed together in the right amounts with a *hin* of oil produced the anointing compound that was called holy. It was the mixture that was considered holy. The Lord combines all the good and difficult things in your life with the oil of the Holy Spirit. A sweet anointing then forms in you, and He'll be able to use you in incredible ways.

> *But the anointing which you have received from Him abides in you, and you do not need that anyone teach you; but as the same anointing teaches you concerning all things, and is true, and is not a lie, and just as it has taught you, you will abide in Him* (1 John 2:27).

One of the greatest problems is the thinking that you can live any way you please, and then when you come to witness, preach, or minister you can simply ask God for an anointing. Then after it is over you can go back to being your normal unspiritual self. Not true—there is a price to pay to carry a high level of anointing!

The anointing is a sign of God's approval over God's chosen vessels. Remember King Saul lost his anointing to be king because of his disobedience. His disobedience stemmed from his desire to please people rather than do what God had commanded. Just as the spices were costly and rare, so is the price you pay to have the anointing abide in your life. He will qualify you!

We have to ask ourselves how we will carry the weight of His Glory in our lives. Just imagine you are a Hebrew out walking on a hot day. Down the road you see what looks like a cow pulling a cart with some object. The sun is reflecting off the object and is creating a brilliant glow. As it comes closer you realize that it is the Ark of the Covenant, which was lost in battle seven months ago. Eli's sons, Hophni and Phinehas, had taken the ark into battle and both had been slain. The ark was captured by the Philistines. Now it is heading down the road right toward you.

In the ark was the law, showing that the law must be written in our hearts. Then it held the manna that did not rot or mildew, showing us that we must feed on the bread of life. It also contained Aaron's rod that budded without the need of earth.

The Philistines had taken the ark from city to city, and at each of their five cities plagues had broken out. So finally they decided to see if it was the ark of God that was causing their troubles. They build a new cart and placed a cow in front to pull it. This cow had just had a calf and they knew that the cow's natural instinct was to turn around and head for the calf.

They thought that if she took it toward Israel then they would know that the God of Israel was causing their troubles.

The Philistines had no fear of God! They had opened the ark and 50,000 people were killed for looking inside it. So now the cow was pulling the cart toward Israel. This new cart is an illustration of the new liberalism that causes compromises in the church today.

Once the ark reached Israel, the Jews took the ark and used the wood from the cart to sacrifice the cow to God. The ark was left at that location and remained there during all the years of King Saul.

After David became king, he decided that he wanted the Glory of God in Jerusalem. He wanted the praises of God in Jerusalem. When the Glory is present, then God is home. You don't need a tee shirt or bumper sticker to let the devil know that you are carrying the Glory. The Glory prostrates your soul. David wanted this glory in Zion.

David tried to bring the Glory of God back to Zion (a type of the Church) in a new cart, but not in holiness (see 2 Sam. 6). He tried the world's way to carry the Glory. The new cart was a Philistine idea. The church has become so user friendly, it is compromising its standards and holiness. Do not align yourself with those who shout out the glory and the next day listen to those who tell dirty jokes. Be careful how you carry the weight of the Glory, how you carry the gift of the Holy Spirit. David tried the Philistine way and it cost a man his life.

Uzzah reached up to steady the ark as the oxen stumbled and God struck him down. You have to do it God's way. The Lord doesn't need your help. He had told Israel how to carry the ark over 400 years before. Time does not change God's Word or standards! The full weight of God's glory requires reverence of Him and intercession and repentance. If you want to carry the ark you cannot be doing things in darkness that pollute your soul. There is a cost to carrying the Glory of God in your life.

When David found out that God was blessing the house of Obed-Edom, he decided again to bring the ark back to Jerusalem. This time he found out that the ark was to be carried by God's servants, the Levites. This time they placed the ark upon the shoulders of the Levites and started down the road for Jerusalem. Every six steps the priests would stop, and they would sacrifice an animal. They followed this system all the way to Jerusalem.

Sacrifice, sacrifice, and sacrifice is required to carry the glory of God. Dying to yourself, repentance, and commitment. "*...Be ye clean [holy], that bear the vessels of the Lord*" (Isa. 52:11 KJV). Holiness is a standard God established many years ago for His leaders. God Himself dwells in holiness, and He states that He is holy.

John tells us that we cannot be sinless. But when we do sin, we have a choice: We can live in our sin or we can repent and confess our sin and be forgiven. God promises to cast our sins away as far as the east is from the west.

1 John 1:8-10: *If we say that we have no sin, we deceive ourselves, and the truth is not in us. If we confess our sins, He is faithful and just to forgive us our sins and to cleanse us from all unrighteousness. If we say that we have not sinned, we make Him a liar, and His word is not in us.*

1 John 3:9: *Whoever has been born of God does not sin, for His seed remains in him; and he cannot sin, because he has been born of God.*

1 John 5:18: *We know that whoever is born of God does not sin; but he who has been born of God keeps himself, and the wicked one does not touch him.*

While First John 3:9 and 5:18 seem to imply that we should never sin, this is not John's meaning. He is stating that those who are children of God do not indulge in habitual sins. When we are indulging in habitual sin then we are disqualifying ourselves and walking out from under our anointing as leaders.

If you have felt ministered to by any chapter in this book and feel you may fit into one of these categories that God speaks about, then the answer is simple. Go to prayer before the loving Father God and ask for His forgiveness.

He will cleanse and restore you in His service. He is the God of second chances. When Peter denied Him, Jesus went to him and restored him. When David failed God, he was given a second chance. God loves you and wants you serving Him in the calling that He has placed upon your life.

REVIEW QUESTIONS

1. What does the word *anointing* mean?

2. Would God accept the anointing oil if any ingredient were missing?

3. What does the spice myrrh represent in the anointing?

4. Why do you think God included cinnamon in the oil?

AUTHOR MINISTRY PAGE

Bishop Farley can be contacted at:

Martinsburg Christian Center
PO Box 457, Inwood, WV
Phone: 1-304-263-6209

www.martinsburgchristiancenter.com